Romantic Days and Nights®
in Houston

Help Us Keep This Guide Up to Date

Every effort has been made by the author and editors to make this guide as accurate and useful as possible. However, many things can change after a guide is published—establishments close, phone numbers change, facilities come under new management, etc.

We would love to hear from you concerning your experiences with this guide and how you feel it could be improved and kept up to date. Although we may not be able to respond to all comments and suggestions, we'll take them to heart and we'll make certain to share them with the author. Please send your comments and suggestions to the following address:

The Globe Pequot Press
Reader Response/Editorial Department
P.O. Box 480
Guilford, CT 06437

Or you may e-mail us at:
editorial@globe-pequot.com

Thanks for your input,
and happy travels!

ROMANTIC DAYS AND NIGHTS® SERIES

Romantic Days and Nights®

IN HOUSTON

Romantic Diversions
in and around the City

by Margaret Luellen Briggs

The Globe Pequot Press

GUILFORD, CONNECTICUT

Cover illustration, text design, and interior illustrations by M.A. Dubé
Spot art by www.ArtToday.com
Maps by Mary Ballachino

Library of Congress Cataloging-in-Publication Data
Briggs, Margaret Luellen.
      Romantic days and nights in Houston : romantic diversions in and
   around the city / by Margaret Luellen Briggs.—1st ed.
         p. cm. — (Romantic days and nights series)
      Includes index.
      ISBN 0-7627-0710-0
      1. Houston Region (Tex.)—Guidebooks. 2. Couples—Travel—Texas—
   Houston Region—Guidebooks. I. Title. II. Series.

F394.H83 B75 2000
917.64'1411—dc21
                                                                    00-034821

Manufactured in the United States of America
First Edition/First Printing

To book lovers and globetrotters,
with heartfelt appreciation.

Acknowledgments

Thanks to my husband, my family, and my dear friends, whose seemingly limitless patience and support I can never repay; and to the long-suffering editors and professors who put up with my high-wire schedule juggling act. Special thanks to my "road warrior" companions who cheerfully trekked along on research expeditions near and far, and to Lisa Gray, who not only believed I could do it but showed me how.

Contents

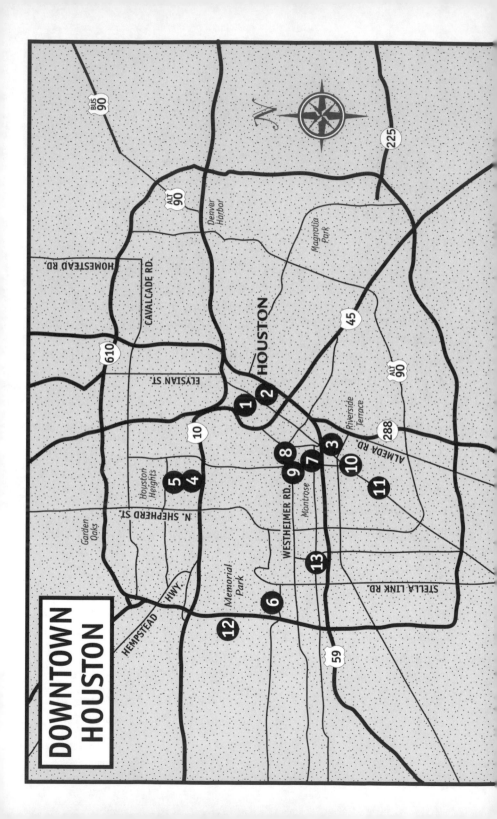

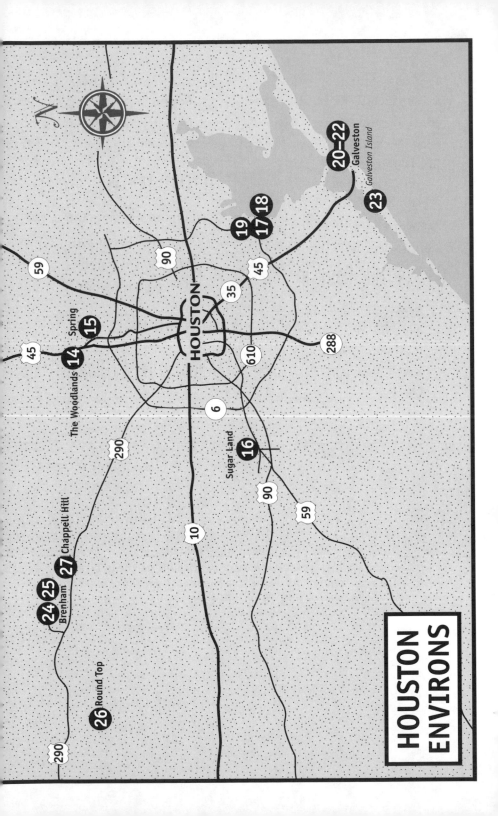

HOUSTON
ENVIRONS

*The prices and rates
listed in this guidebook were confirmed at press time.
We recommend, however, that you call establishments
before traveling to obtain current information.*

Introduction

IRST-TIMERS EXPECT THE WILD, WILD WEST when they come to Houston, a Hollywood-inspired pastiche of dashing Stetson'ed cowboys, dusty longhorn steers, and ice-cold, long-neck beers. And sure enough, every February the city truly does look like a *Lonesome Dove* movie set. During the annual live-stock show and rodeo, one of the largest in the world, Houstonians gleefully and completely "go Texan." Others seek and find the legendary big bucks of the "oil bidness" that built the city; a land of sleek limousines, bejeweled matrons, and jaw-dropping mansions, monuments to success, even excess.

But our Gulf Coast cityscape actually has more in common with the slow soul of the Deep South: Think antebellum estates fronting lazy bayous, spreading live oak trees draped in Spanish moss, and lush green lawns bordered every spring with brilliant azalea blooms. Greenbelts and parks beckon, and glorious spring and fall weather lures Houstonians outdoors in droves to jog and bike and sail, to attend theater and musical performances under the stars, and to linger late on moonlit dining patios and decks. Summers here are as sultry as can be, but when the entire city boasts polar-blast air-conditioning, who cares? Even the office workers of downtown's glittering skyscrapers bustle through miles of comfortably cool underground tunnels lined with shops and restaurants.

THE ITINERARIES

Considering that Houston is the nation's fourth-largest city, its four million greater metropolitan residents spread over some 75 miles north to south and again east to west, it's surprising that it's also one of this country's least-discovered destinations for lovers. Even our otherwise knowledgeable native Houstonian friends scoffed at the notion of a book full of local itineraries for romance. Shoot, it was a snap! We started with four-star hotels and luxurious resorts, added culinary thrills and glamorous shopping, and found dozens of getaways just perfect for lovers of luxury. We sought out elegant little bed-and-breakfasts in pretty, peaceful neighborhoods, explored the world-class museums and operatic companies nearby, and designed weekend escapes to satisfy the most demanding art devotees. And for adventure lovers what treats are in store! You two can prowl offbeat art galleries and eccentric coffeehouses, gain admittance to avant-garde performances, and maybe spy an "art car" or two.

So our pages were already half-filled before leaving the city limits, or even straying far outside Houston's famous Loop 610, which geographically divides the inner city from the outer. Then we hit the road. Just north of town we found luxurious wooded resorts, quiet family farms, historical villages, and quaint shops to explore hand in hand. We went south to Clear Lake, which is neither clear nor a lake but a great venue for sailing, shopping, and dining. Stay southbound to revel in the warm waters of the Gulf of Mexico, lapping the shores of Galveston Island: Only an hour's drive from Houston's central business district are sun-worshippers' beaches galore, lovingly restored Victorian homes, classic sailing ships, and horsedrawn carriages. To the northwest the green rolling hills of Brenham, Chappel Hill, and Round Top offer a serene, country getaway complete with bluebonnets, antique roses, and antiques stores, to say nothing of the "best ice cream in the country"; to the southwest Brazos Bend State Park offers a chance to reacquaint yourselves with nature and each other, with a magnificent observatory for stargazing.

Using This Book

Our itineraries are designed with a weekend's leisure in mind, most adventures starting on Friday afternoons and dallying through lazy Sundays. You can, of course, mix and match your romantic options as you see fit. You'll find great notions for a first-date evening or a day trip perfect for an anniversary surprise. Many of the neighborhoods we explore are quite close to one another, like the Museum District, Montrose, and West University, for example. Don't hesitate to match a romantic restaurant from one itinerary with love-nest lodgings from another. Although hotel and bed-and-breakfast prices can fluctuate seasonally, especially in summertime favorite resort areas like Galveston and Clear Lake, you'll be pleased to find that rates compare very favorably with other tourist destinations.

Restaurants

Food critics have declared Houston an international gourmand's paradise, and with some 4,000 restaurants dishing out cuisine from all over the globe, it's easy to see why. Sure, you'll find world-famous Tex-Mex and barbecue bar none, but Houston restaurants also speak with sultry *Nuevo Latino*, sophisticated pan-Asian, and cutting-edge "New American" accents. In keeping with Houston's subtropical climate and blessedly unpretentious mindset, very few establishments, even the most select, require dressing to the nines. But the best news is this: Our dining prices are astonishingly low. According to the Zagat restaurant survey, a three-course meal complete with a well-chosen glass of wine averages little more than $17. No wonder Houstonians dine out almost five times a week! Our price ratings tell you what to expect, with "inexpensive" options tallying under $20, "moderate" falling between $20 and $40, and "expensive" ranging from $40 and up, per person.

Speaking of prices, the pleasant little piggy bank icon you'll see scattered throughout the book indicates a particularly good buy, ideal for lovers on a budget.

Getting Here and Getting Around

Houston has two major airports, Bush Intercontinental and Hobby. Intercontinental is on the north side of town, about a forty-five-minute ride from downtown; Hobby, on the southeast side, is usually no more than fifteen minutes from downtown by cab. Of course, a lot depends on traffic, an infamous factor in Houston, particularly during weekday rush hours. It's a shame our public transportation system isn't more extensive outside the downtown area; plan on using a car to traverse our sprawling 600-square-mile metropolis. Once you've arrived at many of our destinations, though, you can park your car and forget it for the weekend, safely strolling, biking, or even roller blading—why not?—within neighborhoods.

FOR MORE INFORMATION

Greater Houston Convention and Visitor's Center
901 Bagby
Houston, TX 77002
(713) 227–3100
(800) 4HOUSTON
www.houston-guide.com

Brenham Chamber of Commerce
314 South Austin Street
Brenham, TX 77834
(979) 836–3695
(888) BRENHAM
www.brenhamtexas.com

Galveston Convention & Visitor Bureau
2106 Seawall Boulevard
Galveston, TX 77550
(409) 763–4311
(888) 425–4753
www.galveston.com

Clear Lake Area Chamber of Commerce
1201 East Nasa Road One
Houston, TX 77058
(281) 488–7676
www.clearlakearea.com

The Best of Houston

The Most Romantic Lodgings

Ant Street Inn

Browning Plantation

Captain's Quarters

Heart of My Heart Ranch

La Colombe d'Or Hotel

Lancaster Hotel

McLachlan Farm Bed & Breakfast

Robin's Nest Bed & Breakfast

Sara's Bed & Breakfast Inn

Sculpture Garden Tranquil Bed N Breakfast

Ten Best Bets for Culture Lovers

Cynthia Woods Mitchell Pavilion

Da Camera Chamber Music Society

Festival-Institute at Round Top

Galleries on Colquitt Street (several)

Menil Collection Museum

Museum District

Opera in the Heights

Rothko Chapel

Stages Repertory Theatre

Theater District

Five Sexiest Night Spots

Cezanne

Jones Bar

Marfreless

Mercury Room

Mo Mong

Five Best Sunset Views

Aboard Star Fleet Yachts or the *Lady Christina*

King Biscuit Café

Observation Deck of the Chase Tower

Sonoma Restaurant

Scott Gertner's Skybar

Ten Best Places for Culinary Feasts

Americas

Boulevard Bistrot

Brazos Belle

Churrasco's

Daily Review Café

De Ville

Mark's

Royers' Round Top Café

Tony Ruppe's Fine American Food and Wine

Urbana

Five Most Romantic Restaurants

La Mora Cucina Toscana

La Tour d'Argent

Rainbow Lodge

Tutto Bene

Villa Capri

Five Best Places for Pampering Body and Soul

Four Seasons Hotel

The St. Regis Hotel

The Warwick Hotel

The Houstonian Hotel, Club & Spa

The Woodlands Executive
Conference Center and Resort

Five Best-Loved Offbeat Scenes

Art Car Museum

La Carafe

Last Concert Café

The Orange Show

No Tsu Oh Coffee House

Five Most Romantic Photo Opportunities

Bayou Bend Collection and Gardens

Bluebonnet Tours around Brenham

Lovett Hall at Rice University

North and South Boulevards in West University

The Water Wall at Williams Tower Park

Five Best Places to Savor Sweets for the Sweet

Andre's Tea Room and Swiss Pastry Shop

Blue Bell Creameries

Cheesecake Factory

Dessert Gallery Bakery & Café

Dolce & Freddo

Five Most Perfect Picnic Spots

Antique Rose Emporium

Brazos Bend State Park

Buffalo Bayou Park

Houston Arboretum and Nature Center

Miller Outdoor Theater

Five Best Places to Dance the Night away

410

Billy Blues BBQ Bar & Grill

Los Andes

Seabrook Beach Club

What's Cookin Restaurant

Urban Arts and Adventures

Downtown

La Dolce Vita

OUSTON'S DOWNTOWN DISTRICT has undergone an astonishing renaissance in the last few years, and now a rising tide of diners and dancers throngs downtown's sidewalks most every night of the week. The glittering hub of all this excitement is Houston's **Theater District**, the 4-block area that's home to six world-class performing arts companies: the **Houston Grand Opera** (713–546–0200), the **Houston Ballet** (713–523–6300), the **Houston Symphony** (713–224–4240), the **Alley Theater** (713–228–9341), the **Society for Performing Arts** (713–227–2787), and the **Da Camera** chamber music society (713–524–7601). Nor are these backwater, out-in-the-boonies endeavors: The Houston Ballet is the fifth-largest company in the country, the Alley recently received a Tony for best U.S. regional theater, and the Houston Grand Opera has garnered triple-crown kudos, with multiple Grammy, Tony, *and* Emmy awards.

And only 1 block away, glitzy Bayou Center is alive with nightlife choices, including live music from national acts at the Aerial Theater and first-run movies at the ten-screen Angelika Film Center. Whew!

This itinerary is designed for all you culture lovers, darlings, for whom life without theater, champagne, and caviar is simply not worth living. If, for you, the most thrilling sound in the world is the expectant hush just before the curtain rises, this weekend will be sheer heaven.

PRACTICAL NOTES: You'll need to book your tickets before starting your trip. The problem, you'll find, is not so much getting your pair of tickets as it is choosing which of a dozen shows you

Romance AT A GLANCE

◆ Lounge in the lap of understated luxury at the **Lancaster Hotel** (701 Texas Avenue; 713–228–9500), in the heart of Houston's Theater District. Your pretheater supper is conveniently close, at the hotel's acclaimed **Bistro Lancaster** (713–228–9502).

◆ Take in a show of your choice; then stroll to one of downtown's swankiest nightspots, the **Mercury Room** (1008 Prairie at Main; 713–225–6372), for champagne and caviar and a little night music for close dancing.

◆ Take a daylight walking tour of the Theater District, exploring **Sesquicentennial Park** for a romantic backdrop to your souvenir photographs. Continue to **Bayou Center** for a friendly game of billiards at **Slick Willie's Family Pool Hall** (560 Texas; 713–225–1277), followed by a light lunch at **Mingalone Italian Bar and Grill** (540 Texas; 713–223–0088) or the dramatic **Sake Lounge** (500 Texas; 713–228–7253). After lunch check out the heart-fluttering view of Houston from the lofty observation deck of our tallest skyscraper, the **Chase Tower** (Texas Street at Travis).

◆ Find candlelit amore over an early supper at **Buca Di Bacco** (700 Milam; 713–224–2426) before your next theater engagement.

◆ Indulge in a decadently rich Sunday brunch at Bistro Lancaster and then take in an afternoon matinee at the **Angelika Film Center and Café** (510 Texas, in Bayou Place; 713–225–1609). For a special treat afterward, try a heaping plate of Texas barbecue to the sweet strains of live gospel music at **Harlon's Bayou Blues** (530 Texas; 713–230–0111).

want to see. Start by reviewing the Theater District schedule on the Greater Houston Convention and Visitors Bureau Web site at www.houston-guide.com/guide/arts/artsschedule.html or call the *Houston Chronicle* Arts Line at (713) 220–2000, access code 2787 (ARTS).

Next, contact the Wortham Ticket Center at (713) 227–ARTS. The phone folks here are well informed and helpful, ready to assist you in choosing seats for the opera or the ballet or in routing your call to the symphony and the Society for Performing Arts. You can also contact the individual box offices directly at the numbers given above, or you can purchase tickets from Ticketmaster at (713) 629–3700. Prepare to be pleasantly surprised by the bargain pricing of Houston arts venues compared with those of other major cities.

Weekend ballet seats start as low as $11.50 and grand opera seats at $32.00; card-carrying seniors and students can often get deep discounts on the day of the show.

DAY ONE: evening

Your home this weekend is the elegant little **Lancaster Hotel** (701 Texas Avenue; 713–228–9500; rooms $130 to $325, suites $450 to $1,000). Not only is its location at the corner of Louisiana Street and Texas Avenue ideal for your theater plans, the hotel itself is a real gem, an oasis of understated luxury in English country-house style. You'll immediately see why Condé Nast *Traveler* magazine called the Lancaster "one of the best places to stay in the world." Uniformed bellmen greet you at the gleaming brass-and-glass doors and usher you into a plush interior of polished antiques and fresh flowers. You'll revel in the white-glove service: The Lancaster's concierges stand ready to help you obtain theater tickets or dinner reservations, while the complimentary downtown shuttle service is at your beck and call (not that you'll need a ride—everything worth doing this weekend is within easy, safe, and well-lit walking distance).

The Lancaster offers a honeymoon package that bundles breakfast for two, champagne and chocolate-dipped strawberries, and valet parking with a deluxe room ($200) or a one-bedroom suite ($325). Every room is attractively furnished, boasting marble baths and an armoire concealing the TV, video, and stereo system, but we're particularly fond of those rooms that end in "02" on each of the Lancaster's nine floors. These light and airy corner rooms offer a stunning view of Theater Plaza below.

DINNER

As you check in this evening, go ahead and request your dinner reservations at the hotel's intimate street-level restaurant, the **Bistro Lancaster** (701 Texas; 713–228–9502; expensive). Shall we say six-ish, so you're sure to make your curtain? The Bistro is quite popular with theater lovers like you, as you'll find, and hushed enough for truly private conversations. The room is lovely, decorated in soothing tones of hunter green trimmed with glossy wood and brass, but executive chef Tommy Child's "neo–Gulf Coast" cuisine is the real draw. For starters try the crabmeat quesadilla with salsa verde; for dinner perhaps the pecan-crusted rack of venison with jalapeño-herb demiglace, or the chili-rubbed pork tenderloin bathed in rich mole sauce. Then just try to resist the dessert lineup with seductive contenders like the warm croissant bread pudding with dried cherries, fig coulis, caramel sauce, and crème fraiche, or the Bananas Lancaster, sporting bananas caramelized in brandy, served on vanilla cake, and laved with roasted-banana-cream sauce. You'd better get two spoons for each dish and share the delicacies bite by bite.

Afterward take your loved one's arm and stroll elegantly to your show. No matter which Theater District venue you've chosen, it's sure to be within a block or two of your hotel. Congratulate yourselves on your cleverness as you pass double lines of cars crowding into those stuffy underground parking garages.

We've never liked going straight home after a show, and neither should you. The night is young, and you're well dressed. Why not saunter 4 blocks to one of downtown's sexiest new nightspots, the **Mercury Room** (1008 Prairie at Main; 713–225–6372). You'll gasp at the ceiling-high bar stocked with all sorts of liquid goodies, aged cognacs and Armagnac and such, but we think a flute of bubbly goes best with the Mercury's outrageous selection of Russian and American caviars. Sink into an overstuffed, under-lit couch and feed each other precious salty roe from tiny horn spoons, or hit the downstairs dance floor, where sultry blues and jazz keep you circling cheek to cheek and hip to hip.

DAY TWO: morning

BREAKFAST

Take your time getting started this morning; you've earned a luxurious lie-in. You might dress and go downstairs for breakfast at the Bistro Lancaster, or you might simply phone room service. It's your choice, and you've got until the civilized hour of 11:00 A.M. to make up your minds. Either way, we recommend the Bistro's eye-opening take on eggs Benedict, called the Lancaster: two poached eggs on a toasted English muffin with grilled Virginia ham and tomatoes, decadently drenched in hollandaise sauce. Too rich, you virtuous duo? Then how about johnnycakes—fetchingly light cornmeal pancakes—with fresh berry coulis, instead? You'll never believe this concoction weighs in at under two grams of fat.

This morning we recommend you two take a walking tour of the **Theater District, Sesquicentennial Park,** and the nearby **Bayou Center.** It all looks very different by day, and you're sure to see more than you did last night, when you only had eyes for each other.

From the Lancaster walk 1 block over to the **Wortham Theater Center** (500 Texas; 713–237–1439), just past the turreted concrete-castle facade of the **Alley Theater** (615 Texas; 713–228–8421). Unless you were here last night, prepare to be astonished. From its handsome door pulls to its towering columns festooned with sculpted, multicolored ribbons, this center is a stunner. As you two float up, up, up the breathtaking length of escalator, you'll surely feel you're rising into Elysian fields of music.

Just beyond the Wortham the ten-acre **Sesquicentennial Park** slopes gently down to the slow-moving waters of Buffalo Bayou, beckoning you to explore. Seven 70-foot-tall steel pillars are charmingly decorated with the artwork of Houston schoolchildren, at night lit from within for better viewing. The plaza, with its three-story pavilion, ornamental cascades, and spreading floral gardens, makes a great backdrop for photos; set the timer and pose together. Follow one of the many trails to find a secluded spot to embrace your beloved.

Then proceed 2 blocks down Smith Street to the **Bayou Center** (on Smith Street between Texas Avenue and Capitol Street). Stop by the **Aerial Theater** (520 Texas; 713–230–1666) to see what's playing tonight. This surprisingly intimate venue for pop music and comedy holds as many as 3,000 fans; recent performances have ranged from Smashing Pumpkins and Jethro Tull to Weird Al Yankovic and Jeff Foxworthy. The box office, which opens at 10:00 A.M. on Saturdays, is also a full-service Ticketmaster outlet, in case you're seeking seats somewhere else.

Around the front, or Smith Street side, of Bayou Place, you'll find the **Angelika Film Center and Cafe** (510 Texas in Bayou Place;

713–225–1609), a gorgeous art-house cinema with a breezy sidewalk cafe that's ideal for people-watching day or night. Check the schedule for a romantic movie this afternoon or in case you'd like to come back for a Sunday afternoon matinee. If you're feeling a bit peckish, you might take a seat under one of the umbrellas and order a pastry and cappuccino to tide you over until lunch. Lean close together and watch the world go by.

Or head upstairs to **Slick Willie's Family Pool Hall** (560 Texas; 713–225–1277), which, as its name protests, is not a dark smoky den of juvenile delinquents, but a well-lit place for good, clean fun. Check out the giant eight ball at the entrance and the surprisingly good view over Theater Plaza from its second-story windows. Play at pool shark: Challenge your charmer to a friendly game of billiards, betting kisses—or more serious favors—to be exchanged later, in private.

DAY TWO: afternoon

LUNCH

Start eyeing likely places for lunch before hunger strikes. We're fond of the industrial-luxe look and feel of the **Mingalone Italian Bar and Grill** (540 Texas in Bayou Place; 713–223–0088; moderate). The menu is perfect for upscale snacking—try the fried calamari or Italian sausages—and the frozen Bellinis are outstanding. Perhaps even more fun is the dramatic **Sake Lounge** (500 Texas; 713–228–7253; moderate), praised as one of America's best new restaurants when it opened in 1998, and home to light lunch combinations with a sexy Asian flair. Sushi, we're convinced, is a natural aphrodisiac, so indulge yourselves in some impeccably fresh yellowfin or spicy salmon. When the weather's fine, the outdoor patios of both restaurants are divine for al fresco dining.

You'll complete your strolling tour of downtown with a bird's-eye view of the city from the observation deck of its tallest skyscraper. From Bayou Place walk southeast along Capitol Street. You're heading away from the bayou, if that helps your mental compasses any. (Visitors often complain that downtown's grid isn't aligned to a true north/south axis; certainly it would be simpler, but instead Houston's forefathers oriented our streets to run parallel and perpendicular to the bayou.)

At Capitol and Louisiana tip your heads back to admire the steep, spiky roofline of the pinkish-stone **NCNB Center** designed by architects Philip Johnson and John Burgee, inspired by the Dutch Renaissance. Look into the lobby, too; it's awesome. In the next block you'll spy the black glass **Pennzoil Place** at Milam and Capitol, whose twin towers were also designed by Johnson and Burgee. It's rumored the boys were drinking martinis and playing with matchboxes when inspiration struck for this one. This is also the site for your pretheater supper this evening, at cozy little **Buca Di Bacco** on the ground floor. Inside the Pennzoil lobby you can also peek into the **Barbara Davis Gallery** (711 Louisiana; 713–236–0600). Open by appointment only, this salon houses a subset of Davis's eclectic collection of contemporary art, representing Texas, American, and international artists.

Now turn left on Travis Street and proceed 1 block northeast to Texas Street to find the **Chase Tower,** at seventy-five stories the tallest building in Houston. This five-sided edifice is sited diagonally on its block to accommodate a small plaza in front, dominated by Joan Miró's powerful sculpture called *Personage with Birds.* Look up: The upper floors of the building may be wreathed in clouds. If not, proceed to the **Observation Deck** on the sixtieth floor. We assume you'll want to take the elevator, but some prefer the stairs. Stair-climbing champion Rich Yanacek raced up them in seven minutes, thirteen seconds (he was forty years old at the time, mind you).

However you get there, the western-facing view of Houston's sprawling cityscape is astonishing. Look for the silvery hemisphere of the **Astrodome** and the striking spire of the **Williams Energy Tower** at the Galleria (still stubbornly called the Transco Tower by most Houstonians). Chances are you'll have the place to yourselves on weekends, so seize the opportunity for kisses sky-high above the city.

It's only 3 blocks back to your hotel northwest along Texas Street, so when you've admired your fill, stroll slowly home. Perhaps a power nap is in order. Draw the thick drapes, turn on some soft music, and relax into each other's arms.

DAY TWO: evening

DINNER

Refreshed and renewed from your late-afternoon siesta, you'll be ready to return to Pennzoil Place for an early supper at **Buca Di Bacco** (700 Milam; 713–224–2426; moderate). The best Italian dishes at this unpretentious family-owned restaurant are the pasta plates or the fresh seafood numbers, like the cozze marinara (mussels in tomato sauce) for starters, followed by the rich house-made ravioli for an entree, or the linguine vongole alla Francese with clams in a white-wine sauce. Desserts vary at the chef's whim, so you might consider tiramisù, zabaglione, or a plate of dainty cream puffs drenched in warm chocolate. For a very special ending to your meal, ask about the secret-recipe digestif of the house, a light, lemony elixir that will bring a glow to your cheeks and a sparkle to the eyes of your loved one. Afterward it's a short stroll to your evening's entertainment in the Theater District.

The Music of Love

What's your idea of sexy music to love by? Would it be Barry White (a la Allie McBeal) or the kinder, gentler crooning of Marvin Gaye? Willie Nelson's "Stardust" or Sinatra's "Ol' Blue Eyes"? Buddy Holly "It's So Easy" or Bob Dylan "Lay, Lady, Lay"? Put your heads together and pack a romantic mood-setting CD selection for this weekend that's just right for the two of you, and don't forget to include "your song."

DAY THREE: morning

BREAKFAST

One of downtown's best Sunday brunches is oh-so-conveniently ready and waiting at the Lancaster's Bistro; aren't you glad? You two can lounge late abed, browse the thick Sunday newspaper, then dress for this weekend's farewell meal. The Bistro brunch is served a la carte, with tempting menu choices like tequila-smoked salmon, scrambled-egg popovers, and croissant French toast, loaded with strawberries and bathed in roasted-banana cream.

Afterward you can return to the **Angelika Film Center and Café** (510 Texas, in Bayou Place; 713–225–1609) for an early-afternoon matinee. The cinemas are cool and dark and generally almost deserted on Sundays: You'll have plenty of privacy for cuddling and other sweet indiscretions.

Just around the corner from the cinema in Bayou Place you'll find primo Texas-style barbecue at **Harlon's Bayou Blues** (530 Texas; 713–230–0111; inexpensive), served in kicked-back cafeteria style at lunchtime. Barbecue patriarch Harlon Brooks has a special treat in store for you most Sundays, when he turns his rustic ribs joint into a showcase for live gospel music in the afternoon and jazz in the early evening. Linger as long as you like, tapping your feet and sipping cold, long-neck beers. You'll wish Monday would never come.

$\mathcal{D}$owntown

THE SPORTING LIFE

*T*HERE'S MORE TO DOWNTOWN LIFE than the highbrow arts, you'll be delighted to learn. The centerpiece of this itinerary is a baseball game at Houston's gorgeous new field of dreams, the **Ballpark at Enron Field.** Before and after the ball game, your revelries will revolve around downtown's hottest development nexus, the former Rice Hotel—now called the **Rice Lofts,** but better known simply as "The Rice"—that's been rejuvenated as posh, utterly urban condominiums chock-a-block with nightclubs, restaurants, and shops at street level.

Best of all, you won't ever have to fight for that downtown rarity, a parking space. Deliver your car to the tender mercies of the valets at the Four Seasons on Friday afternoon and forget about it for the rest of the weekend. You'll wander everywhere you like afoot, or you can ride Metro's picturesque trolley cars (for free!).

PRACTICAL NOTES: You'll want to plan your trip around the regular season schedule of the **Houston Astros** (1301 McKinney Street; 713–799–9567) between April and September, as playoff tickets in October are darned hard to come by. Ticket prices range from $1.00 for the outfield deck to $29.00 for down-and-dirty dugout seating; you can also obtain tickets from Ticketmaster (713–629–3700). This itinerary is designed with a Saturday-afternoon game in mind, but you can easily customize it for a game on Friday night.

Romance
AT A GLANCE

◆ Prepare to be pampered at the sophisticated **Four Seasons Hotel** *(1300 Lamar Street; 713–650–1300), a dyna-mite combo of hotel and urban spa facili-ties. Drop off your bags and warm up for your sports-themed weekend with a subterranean exploration of Houston's vast tunnel system from* **Discover Houston Tours** *(713–222–9255).*

◆ *Resurface just in time for happy hour and sip a genteel cocktail or two at the* **State Bar & Lounge** *(909 Texas; 713–229–8888) in the heart of the thriving* **Rice Hotel** *development.*

◆ *Dine on spicy Tex-Mex, Houston's native cuisine, at the jumpin'* **Cabo Mix-Mex Grill** *(419 Travis; 713–225–2060) or the calmer environs of* **Cantina Tres Caballos** *(502 Main; 713–221–1695). In either case you'll down some world-class margaritas.*

◆ *Then put on your party hats for a club-hopping tour of downtown hotspots:* **Solero** *and* **Swank** *(910 Prairie Street; 713–227–2665) and* **Jones Bar** *and* **410** *(410 Main Street; 713–225–6637).*

◆ *Recuperate with a spa morning of massage and sauna; then lunch before the game at* **Mission Burritos** *(909 Texas at Main; 713–224–1440) or* **Liberty Noodles** *(713–222–BOWL). Stop by* **Amy's Ice Cream** *for a double scoop, then board the trolley for* **Enron Field.**

◆ *Sup in quiet luxury at the Four Seasons's four-star restaurant,* **De Ville** *(1300 Lamar Street; 713–652–6250). Then return to your suite and hang out the* DO NOT DISTURB *sign.*

◆ *Bring your weekend to a smashing close with a Roman-style pasta orgy for Sunday brunch, lubricated by bottomless mimosas or Bellinis at* **Mia Bella Trattoria** *(320 Main, corner of Preston and Main; 713–237–0505).*

Call **Discover Houston Tours** (713–222–9255) to arrange your guided tour "down under" Houston in advance, as well as any other half-day downtown walking tours that strike your fancy.

Other special times for any downtown itinerary include the holiday season and Christmas lighting ceremonies, and the two-week Houston International Festival in April. In the summertime you could kick off your weekend early with the free rock-'n'-roll concert series called Party on the Plaza, held every Thursday night in Jones Plaza across from Bayou Place.

DAY ONE: afternoon

Begin your romantic weekend by checking into the brass-and-marble glamour of the **Four Seasons Hotel** (1300 Lamar Street; 713–650–1300; $155 to $380) near downtown's red-white-and-blue George R. Brown Convention Center complex. Not only is the Four Seasons currently the hotel closest to the **Ballpark at Enron Field,** it's a model of modern creature comforts, including such perks as a personal trainer and full-service spa. The sweetest deal is the Four Seasons's "Romantic Rendezvous" package, available only on weekends for $290 per night. You'll love the handsomely furnished executive suite with spacious sitting area, its king-size bed discreetly tucked into an alcove; frills include a bottle of bubbly and box of chocolate truffles, complimentary valet parking, and a full American breakfast delivered to your bedside each morning from room service.

The first order of business this afternoon is a unique tour of downtown "down under." First-time visitors to Houston's thriving business district are sometimes mystified to see so few people on the sidewalks. That's because the majority of office workers scoot through downtown's **underground tunnel system,** the most extensive such network in the nation. (The air-conditioned comfort is especially welcome in summer, when the thermometer seems permanently stuck somewhere in the upper 90s.) Down under the streets and buildings are 6 miles of shops, restaurants, and services ranging from shoe-resoling to watch repair.

The best time to explore subterranean downtown is on Friday afternoons, when a festive "TGIF" air quickens everyone's steps, and most of downtown's corporate offices follow a casual dress policy. The closest tunnel system entrance is under **The Park Shops** mall (1200 McKinney; 713–759–1442), right across the street from your hotel: Cross the skywalk and follow the escalators down to tunnel level. You can explore the tunnels on your own with maps available from the Downtown District (713–650–3022), several tunnel information desks, or from the downtown Houston Public Library (500 McKinney Street; 713–247–2222). Even with a map it's easy to get lost down there, so we suggest you arrange for a half-day guided tour from **Discover Houston Tours** (713–222–9255), a real bargain at only $10 per couple. Owner Sandra Lord, fondly known locally as the "tunnel lady," will take you on a fascinating warm-up walk around the downtown tunnel loop, culminating in a spectacular preview peek at Enron Field from high above, looking out from the lofty "sky lobby" of the Wells Fargo building. (Ask Lord about other half-day downtown walking tours, like her Heritage Walk or Rice Hotel expedition, which easily combine with the Tunnel Tour for a full day of fun.)

When you emerge from the tunnel system into the **Chase Center** (at the corner of Travis and Texas Streets), the sun should be properly over the yardarm, so proceed immediately across the street to the **State Bar & Lounge** (909 Texas; 713–229–8888) for a happy-hour cocktail, on the second story of the Rice Hotel building. Unlike more frenzied venues at this hour, the State Bar offers a handsome, gimmick-free space for a well-shaken cocktail (no raucous blenders here). If the early evening is fine, sit outdoors on the small terrace; otherwise, relax into a curved, cushy leather couch in the windowed room just off the bar.

DAY ONE: evening

DINNER

Thus fortified, you two will welcome a spicy plateful of Houston's hometown specialty, Tex-Mex cuisine. Or is it an icy salt-rimmed margarita you're craving? Either way, both your hearts' desires will be well satisfied within one city block. We recommend **Cabo Mix-Mex Grill** (419 Travis; 713–225–2060; inexpensive) if you're feeling festive. It's always lively and crowded with pretty people, and it dishes up an addictive fish taco—crisp batter-fried fish fillets tucked into fresh tortillas, decorated with strips of lettuce and red cabbage. Watch out for those killer frozen 'ritas, though; one is usually plenty, and only the strong survive two. If you'd prefer a quieter room with possibly even better food, try **Cantina Tres Caballos** (502 Main; 713–221–1695; moderate) instead; it's right around the corner. Owned by the son of the legendary local restaurateur Ninfa Laurenzo, the draws at this upscale-casual cafe are the sizzling platters of beef, chicken, or shrimp fajitas. The margaritas are fragrant with fresh lime juice, and slightly less lethal than those at Cabo's, you'll be relieved to hear.

Backhanded Compliments

For an exercise in "courtly" love, ask the Four Seasons concierge for guest passes to downtown's members-only **Metropolitan Racquet Club** *(340 West Dallas Street; 713–652–0700). Don your crisp tennis whites, pop a fresh can of balls, and meet at the net on one of the Met's thirteen indoor hard courts. The couple that plays together stays together, unless, of course, one of you plays a golden set. In that case the winner should graciously gift the loser with a sparkling tennis bracelet or gold chain from the conveniently close* **Park Shops in Houston Center** *(1200 McKinney at San Jacinto; 713–759–1442).*

Now you're at ground-zero of Houston's club scene, which really gets cranking around 10:00 P.M. If you'd like to whisk back to the hotel to freshen up and slip into your dancing shoes, there's time. Just hop aboard one of the free Metro trolleys that jingles by every seven minutes. It's only a 10-block ride back to the Four Seasons.

On your return to club land, several very hip nightspots beckon. Pick one or tour several, as your stamina dictates. Start across the street from Cabo at the upstairs/downstairs combination of **Solero** and the **Swank Lounge** (910 Prairie Street; 713–227–2665). Chef Arturo Boada's wildly successful Solero is a Spanish-style tapas bar that actually kicked off this downtown furor when it opened several years ago, and it's even more popular today. Perch at the bar for a cold glass of fruity house-blend sangria and some serious people-watching; then check out the upstairs club action at the Swank Lounge.

Another two-story hotspot is just around the corner at the **Jones Bar** and **410** (410 Main Street; 713–225–6637; weekend cover charge $10). Downstairs, the understated barroom attractively frames the crème de la crème of Houston nightclubbers; velvet ropes at the door keep the Hawaiian shirts and shorts contingent away from the fashion plates. Climb the ominously dark stairs up to

410 and dance, you sexy things, till you're half-deaf from the pulsing neo-disco beat.

Assuming you're ready for bed before the witching hour of 2:00 A.M., jump on a Metro trolley for the ride back to the Four Seasons. (And should you naughty party animals miss that last trolley run, ask the club to summon you a taxicab. Cabbies don't cruise Houston streets as they do in other cities, so a phone call is a must.)

DAY TWO: morning

After last night's rollicking party, you sleepyheads will relish breakfast in bed this morning. An eye-opening cup of steaming hot java, some fresh fruit, and flaky buttered croissants will put a whole new spin on your day. Then we recommend you gird your loins in exercise Lycra and work out last night's kinks and excesses with a morning in the Four Season's exercise facility and spa. That's right, make it burn! Then collapse in a heap in the steamy sauna or schedule a full-body massage to gently bring you back to the land of the living.

DAY TWO: afternoon

LUNCH

Of course you could hold out for the time-honored fan food of hot dogs and peanuts and Cracker Jacks at the ballpark, but life is uncertain so we like to eat lunch first, before that first pitch. Catch the now-familiar trolley car back to the Rice and stoke up on a massive wrap at **Mission Burritos** (909 Texas at Main; 713–224–1440; inexpensive) or a great bowl of steaming pasta-and-veggies at **Liberty Noodles** (713–222–BOWL; inexpensive). You'll still have time to share a hand-packed ice-cream cone at **Amy's Ice Cream** before you board the trolley again or to stroll the 6 blocks to **Enron Field** (corner of Texas and Crawford; 713–227–7971) for the baseball game.

The year 2000 marks the Houston Astros' first season at brand-new Enron Field, a marvel of modern engineering attractively disguised as an old-fashioned bandbox stadium. Check out the glass-walled panoramic view of downtown, the retractable roof above you, and the six acres of real grass down on the field—and how 'bout those 200-foot-long scoreboards? Now it's root, root, root for the home team, and—between spells of jumping up and down and screaming—hug, kiss, hug your partner in thanks for this dream date.

DAY TWO: evening

DINNER

While the echoes of cheers and clapping fade from your ears, tonight we propose something entirely different: a top-notch gourmet meal at **De Ville** (1300 Lamar Street; 713–652–6250; expensive), the world-class restaurant right in your own Four Seasons. We're talking an oasis of white linen, fresh flowers, cut crystal, and white-glove service, on top of one of the best menus and wine lists in town, so do call for reservations.

Executive chef Tim Keating showcases locally grown, seasonally fresh ingredients in masterful assemblages like his porcini glazed veal chop or roasted wild mushroom risotto di Carnarolli. His seasonal "grande" prix-fixe menus are legendary: A recent dinner ran from Maine scallops, lobster and prosciutto ravioli, French roe venison and duck Armagnac sausage, through a artisanal cheese plate and a berry pastry laced with zabaglione, each course matched with gorgeous wines, of course.

After dinner return to your room, turn the lights down low, and pop the cork on that bottle of bubbly. Toast each other and this marvelous weekend and stretch out on the bed for a cable movie. Maybe something adult with an "x" or two in the title, or perhaps something softer and sweeter, instead? You two decide; this is *your* weekend.

DAY THREE: morning

BRUNCH

Draw your weekend to a graceful close with Sunday brunch at **Mia Bella Trattoria** (320 Main, corner of Preston and Main;

713–237–0505; moderate), just a block past the Rice on the trolley route. This attractive windowed room is filled with equally attractive people and the quiet buzz of conversation. Pick and choose from the buffet's generously stocked cold station (delicate smoked salmon, fresh exotic fruits) and hot station (an incredible array of pastas and showboat stuff like tender veal piccata). There's no set menu; the changing selection is entirely up to the very capable chef. You can drown your sweet sorrow at leaving in a bottomless flute of mimosas or Bellinis.

After brunch say a fond farewell to Enron Field with a behind-the-scenes guided tour of the dazzling technology that makes this jewelbox tick. You'll peek into dressing rooms and dugouts, stand at home plate, and view a fascinating film about the stadium's construction in the tour theater. Call **Enron Field** (corner of Texas and Crawford; 713–227–7971) for schedule and prices.

Downtown/ Warehouse District
BOHEMIAN RHAPSODY

WHILE DOWNTOWN HOUSTON PROPER EXPLODES with classy, upscale development, the Warehouse District on its northeast side throbs with activity of a more unconventional sort. Here you'll discover Houston's alternative art and club scene, for some the most compelling and exciting venues in the city. This itinerary features romance with an urban edge, fun and funky, not for the faint of heart or the humorless. Are you two up for unconventional adventures? Then follow us on a journey of self-discovery.

PRACTICAL NOTES: As this itinerary roams farther afield than the other downtown agendas, we recommend you rely on your car rather than public transportation and pack a good street map. Detailed, up-to-date maps of the city are available at **Key Maps, Inc.** (1411 West Alabama Street; 713–522–7949) over in Montrose.

Houston's largest folk-art venue, the **Orange Show,** offers a series of Eyeopeners group tours by bus of the city's exuberant and eccentric homes, galleries, and other art spaces. The most popular tour is the Classic, which includes stops at the Beer Can House, the Flower Man's house, and purple Pigdom; other recent outings have focused on murals and ethnic foods. Any of these freewheeling adventures would complement this itinerary nicely. For more information and reservations, call (713) 926–6368.

The **Patrician Bed and Breakfast** also makes a great base of operations for exploring more conventional art venues at the nearby

Rom**a**n**c**e
AT A GLANCE

♦ Visit an eclectic art venue dedicated to, and run by, Houston artists at the **Lawndale Art Center** (4912 Main Street at Rosedale; 713–528–5858). Then settle in at the **Patrician Bed & Breakfast Inn** (1200 Southmore Boulevard; 800–553–5797 or 713–523–1114), just a few blocks away.

♦ After dinner at Houston's classic Tex-Mex eatery, **Ninfa's on Navigation** (2704 Navigation Boulevard at Canal Street; 713–228–1175), take a pub crawl through the hip watering holes that ring downtown's **Market Square Park.** Stops include the **Market Square Bar & Grill** (311 Travis Street; 713–224–6133), **Warren's Inn** (307 Travis Street; 713–247–9207), and the historic **La Carafe** (813 Congress Street; 713–229–9399). Wind up your evening with coffee and board games at the eccentric **No Tsu Oh Coffee House** (314 Main Street; 713–222–0443).

♦ Spend the morning contemplating citrus at the folk-art extravaganza known as the **Orange Show** (2402 Munger Street; 713–926–6368). Lunch at one of Houston's best Thai cafes, **Kanomwan** (1011 Telephone Road; 713–923–4230); then set off for an eye-opening alternative art tour of the **Warehouse District** just northeast of downtown.

♦ You'll have to knock twice on the red door to be admitted to the **Last Concert Café** (1403 Nance Street; 713–226–8563). Stick around for a live band on the restaurant's tiny patio, open to the stars, or attend an "experimental" theater production on one of the Warehouse District's funky stages. On your way home explore the midtown **open-air flower markets** and pick some pretty posies for your lover.

♦ Take a magical "eye-opening" tour of Houston's folk-art monuments aboard the party bus sponsored by the **Orange Show Foundation** (713–926–6368). Or pack a private picnic lunch and track down some of the show's highlights on your own.

Museum District and the Rice University areas, as detailed in our other itineraries.

DAY ONE: afternoon

To start your explorations, take the Richmond and Wheeler exit from US–59 Downtown and turn right on Main Street, or simply follow Main Street southwest from downtown. The alternative art space at the **Lawndale Art Center** (4912 Main Street at Rosedale; 713–528–5858) is an eye-opening way to set the tone for this weekend's offbeat adventures. This (perhaps surprisingly) upscale gallery is dedicated to the work of Houston artists and also hosts some of the wackiest parties in town, like the wild-and-crazy Hair Ball.

From the Lawndale Art Center, drive 3 blocks southwest on Main—toward the Museum District and Texas Medical Center—and then turn left on Southmore Boulevard. You'll find your home for the weekend, the **Patrician Bed and Breakfast Inn** (1200 Southmore Boulevard; 800–553–5797 or 713–523–1114; $125), at the corner of Southmore and San Jacinto. And you two will feel immediately at home in this stately, yet comfortable mansion.

We like the sunny Margaret Rose suite on the quieter, south side of the house, with its Eastlake antique queen bed and large combination sun porch/sitting room overlooking the garden and gazebo. In this fume-free house, smokers will appreciate the Lollie Dee room for its private outdoor balcony on which to sneak a quick puff; even nonsmokers will admire its view of the downtown skyline.

DAY ONE: evening

DINNER

Ask jaded Houstonians about the Ninfa's chain of Tex-Mex eateries, and they'll probably roll their eyes in frustration. Founded by restaurant matriarch Ninfa Laurenzo and now owned by a franchise-minded partnership, most really aren't worth the trip. The notable exception is **Ninfa's on Navigation** (2704 Navigation Boulevard at Canal Street; 713–228–1175; moderate), the original cafe that has managed to keep its funky charm intact. (Take San Jacinto through downtown, turn right on Franklin, then left on Navigation.) If there's a wait to get in—and there often is, on weekend nights—you can entertain yourselves watching the ladies making tortillas by hand in the front of the restaurant. The sizzling platters of tender, spicy fajitas are still outstanding, and the potent fresh-lime margaritas fuel a constant party in the restaurant's back room. And, oh, that spunky green tomatillo sauce served gratis with salty tortilla chips—you'll just swoon over it.

After dinner you'll drive back into downtown to explore the nightlife opportunities around historic **Market Square Park**, designed in 1836 by Houston's founding duo, the Allen brothers, bounded by Travis, Congress, Milam, and Preston Streets. Parking can be problematic in this area, but resist the temptation to park illegally; speaking from experience, you *will* be towed. We recommend the often-overlooked **Market Square parking garage** on Milam Street next to Kim Son's restaurant, instead.

Start your expedition at the **Market Square Bar & Grill** (311 Travis Street; 713-224-6133), a narrow, high-ceilinged slot of a room next door to Treebeard's restaurant. Proprietor Kent Marshall mixes a wickedly good martini; take your glasses out to the pocket patio in back, an unexpected bit of brick-walled green space between buildings.

A few doors down you'll find **Warren's Inn** (307 Travis Street; 713-247-9207), a real "bar bar," if you know what we mean, smoky and wood paneled. The neon sign and unprepossessing exterior of Warren's made a cameo appearance in the movie *RoboCop*, and the interior has lately been filled with trendy young things and the occasional celebrity.

When you tire of the roar of the crowd at Warren's, slip around the corner to find peace and quiet at **La Carafe** (813 Congress Street; 713-229-9399), which has the double distinction of being Houston's oldest structure as well as the city's most unusual watering hole. (It was built as a bakery in 1845.) It's dimly lit, dusty with history, and irresistibly romantic. Gawk at the enormous knobbly stalagmite of candle wax (or is that a stalactite?) behind the downstairs bar. Wait your turn, if necessary, to climb the creaking wooden stairs to the intimate upstairs bar—it holds about a dozen people, maximum, and feels deliciously private, like a secret treehouse. From this aerie you two can spy on the comings and goings of clubbers in the park below.

Finish your excursion at the wacky **No Tsu Oh Coffee House** (314 Main Street; 713-222-0443)—that's "Houston" spelled backwards, get it? It's a coffeehouse, sure, but it looks more like a combination art gallery and garage sale, furnished with a whimsical collage of cast-off furniture and art constructions. An occasional poetry reading breaks out, and board games abound for your nocturnal entertainment, ranging from chess to Chutes and Ladders. Sink gratefully into a sprung couch or armchair and sip your javas or retire to the thickly cushioned "pillow room," lit by twinkly Christmas lights and screened by dusty curtains from prying eyes. Feel free to lounge as long as you like: The house stays open round-the-clock on weekends.

DAY TWO: morning

Drink your orange juice, every drop, at breakfast in your inn. That's because this morning you're headed out to the **Orange Show** (2402 Munger Street; 713-926-6368), postman Jeff McKissick's sprawling folk-art homage to the noble citrus fruit. Double-check your driving instructions with your hostess since the show can be a little tricky to find, even for natives; then head south on Interstate 45, known locally as the Gulf Freeway. Wander hand in hand through this fantastical landscape of whirligigs, snapping flags, and ceramic-tiled admonitions to "Love Oranges and Live." This site will let both your inner children out to play, we promise.

DAY TWO: afternoon

LUNCH

On your way back from the Orange Show, take the Telephone Road exit from northbound I-45 and turn right, toward downtown. Keep your eyes peeled for a little restaurant called **Kanomwan** (1011 Telephone Road; 713-923-4230; inexpensive), one of Houston's best Thai restaurants. The owner has been compared with Seinfeld's soup Nazi, but under that gruff, growly exterior beats a heart of culinary gold. Dive into a steaming bowl of *tom ka gai* chicken soup, velvety with coconut milk and spiked with lemongrass, or try one of the cafe's trademark Thai curries in red or green. The creamy, ultrastrong iced Thai coffee will stoke your engines for your upcoming adventures.

This afternoon you'll explore the Warehouse District just past downtown, Houston's answer to SoHo. Old historic warehouses, once abandoned, have been recycled into service housing artists' studios, art galleries, and wildly diverse performance spaces. The **Greater Houston Preservation Alliance** (713–216–5000) occasionally organizes "warehouse crawls" of the district, with up to one hundred artists participating; you can also follow our itinerary for a do-it-yourself tour of the same or similar venues. Decide who will drive and who will navigate—this is the perfect partnership effort!—and keep a good street map and your cell phone handy.

You'll start your art prowl on Commerce Street, not quite 3 miles away from the scene of your lunch date. From Kanomwan turn right on Telephone Road, then right again (north) onto South Lockwood Drive. Turn left (west) onto the major artery of Harrisburg Boulevard, then right (northeast) onto Delano Street, and finally left (northwest) onto Commerce Street.

Roughly 4 blocks along Commerce you'll find **Benner Studios** (2327½ Commerce; 713–224–1028), where small, one- or two-artist exhibitions are usually mounted; then proceed to the **Commerce Street Art Warehouse** (2315 Commerce Street; 713–227–3716), one of the best-known venues in this area. Artists of all stripes are at serious work in this rambling, ramshackle warehouse, and the main exhibition gallery mounts a dozen or so large shows a year. The tumbledown theater at the back hosts some, um, interesting productions; a recent crowd-pleaser was the ultracampy *Vampire Lesbians of Sodom*.

Follow Commerce Street to the northwest, crossing under the US–59 elevated, and look for the **Purse Building Studios** (1701 Commerce; 713–228–0635), which showcases the artists who work at the warehouse in its 1,000-square-foot exhibition space. Past the Purse Building, look for the historical Wagon Works Building, which houses **Nancy Littlejohn Fine Arts** (107 Crawford) and the **Wagon Works** exhibition space (101 Crawford).

Continue northeast on Crawford Street and turn left (north) on McKee Street. This route will take you across the **McKee Street Bridge** over Buffalo Bayou, which, when it was built in the 1930s, was the longest such concrete span in the country. In the mid-1980s the bridge was "rescued" from rust and disrepair by a local Houston artist and environmental engineer, Kirk Farris, who painted its curves in luscious shades of aquamarine, lavender, and purple. Farris and other volunteers hauled away trash and landscaped the

surrounding bayou-side acres to make **James Bute Park,** a delightful green space with a superb view of Houston's skyline.

Continue north on McKee Street; then turn right on Rothwell
Street and left on Hardy Street. Then turn left on the Interstate 10
feeder road and make a right on the first street past Walnut Street. This
unmarked street is the entrance to your next stop at **DiverseWorks**
(1117 East Freeway; 713–223–8346), one of the biggest and best
known of these warehouse art venues. Here you may find a poetry
slam in progress, a sexually frank photo exhibit, or a runway
parade of tattooed models. Ask about tonight's scheduled performance—it could be anything, but the thought-provoking plays
mounted by the cutting-edge theater group known as **Infernal
Bridegroom Productions** (713–522–8443) are always worth seeing.

From DiverseWorks backtrack 2 blocks to Nance Street and
check out the gallery space at the **Erie City Ironworks building**
(1302 Nance). The Bridegrooms also play at the nearby **Atomic Café**
(1320 Nance Street; 713–222–2866) in rotation with other equally
art-fringe performance groups. The setting is cramped and stuffy but
draws a delightfully mixed crowd of Houston cognoscenti.

Congratulations! You two sleuths have successfully sniffed out
some of Houston's coolest art venues. You've earned your supper,
which is waiting just down the street.

DAY TWO: evening

DINNER

If your Warehouse District dinner at the **Last Concert Café**
(1403 Nance Street; 713–226–8563; inexpensive) doesn't
make you feel like a Houston insider, nothing will. There's no
sign outside, and you have to know to knock twice on the door to
gain admittance. (Look on the north side of Nance for the festive
courtyard and the number "1403" over the bright red door.) Once
inside, you'll find a charmingly funky dining room decorated in
cheerful watermelon tones of red, white, and green, with an outdoor patio overgrown with banana trees and with a tiny stage that
hosts live music every weekend. Sure, the basic Tex-Mex food's
forgettable, and the margaritas are regrettable (made with wine,
not tequila), but the room and the people are so wonderful you

might just fall in love with this rollicking hangout.

After dinner you can strike out for the performance venue of your choice scouted earlier in the day, or if Carolyn Wonderland is playing tonight at the Last Concert, stick around. She's a wild child who can really belt out some torchy Gulf Coast blues, and there's room for a little dirty dancing in front of the stage or between the patio's picnic tables.

From Nance Street take Rothwell back to San Jacinto, then Fannin, and on through downtown. On the other side of downtown in the neighborhood labeled "midtown" you'll find an amazing collection of brightly lit **open-air flower markets.** These canny vendors decided long ago that it was simpler to stay open all night than to drag their fragrant profusion of bouquets and animal-shaped topiaries in from the sidewalk, so now you can pick posies for your beloved round the clock. Park your car and stroll along the storefronts. Buy a lover's armload of red, red roses or assemble a more exotic bouquet of orchids and birds-of-paradise.

DAY THREE: morning

After a leisurely breakfast at your inn, head back to the **Orange Show** (2402 Munger Street; 713–926–6368) to board the bus for the half-day Eyeopeners tour of your choosing.

Love Note Nosegays

Shy, tongue-tied Victorian lovers left us the language of love expressed in beautiful blooms. Both men and women sent one another bouquets and corsages, each carefully assembled to ask, and answer, "How do I love thee?" Red roses mean "I love you," whereas a white one replies, "I'm worthy." Violets stand for thoughtfulness, white lilies speak of purity and sweetness, and lemon blossoms signify fidelity in love. When assembling your own loving bouquet, though, watch out for those flowers that say "no": You would only give a daylily to a flirt or a narcissus to an egotist, whereas a Michaelmas daisy spells "goodbye."

If your visit doesn't coincide with Eyeopeners, we'll let you in on three of the highlights of Houston eccentricity. Pick up the makings for your own private picnic lunch at the nearby **Butera's Fine Foods & Deli** (4621 Montrose; 713–528–3737), grab your map, and head out. (Remember, these sites are all private homes decorated as a labor of love, so do respect the inhabitants as you unobtrusively admire their heartfelt art from the street.)

You'll find Victoria Herberta's house, called **Pigdom,** on Crawford at Eagle, a purple-hued monument to all that is piggy. With luck, hog-in-residence Jerome will be bathing in his plastic swimming pool out front. If not, admire Ms. Herberta's encyclopedic collection of license plates and soft-drink bottles. Cleveland Turner's home, at 2311 Sauer, is known as **the Flower Man's house**—and you'll see why when you reach this glorious riot of Caribbean color. And you'll hear the **Beer Can House,** at 222 Malone, even before you see it: It's draped with gently tinkling curtains of pull tops recycled from aluminum cans. A retired upholsterer, the late John Milkovisch, painstakingly drained and crushed beer cans to cover the walls of his home. Not only did his loving wife of forty-eight years tolerate his artistic efforts, today she and their two sons keep this strangely beautiful memorial sparkling in his memory.

FOR MORE ROMANCE

After your tour return to the **McKee Street Bridge** and **Bute Park** to spread your blanket for a playful picnic. It's a great spot from which to photograph the downtown skyline and Enron Field or just toss a Frisbee back and forth.

Then sally forth to discover the **Project Row Houses** (2500 Holman Street, at St. Charles and Live Oak Streets; 713–526–7662) in Houston's Third Ward district just west of downtown. Local African-American artists and other volunteers have renovated twenty-two wood-frame "shotgun" houses into an inner city art space. Ten of the houses are dedicated to visual, spoken word, and performance art resonant with meaning for the community. It's an uplifting, inspirational vision of what city life can be and a fitting finale to your weekend's art frolic.

Love and Leisure
inside the Loop

The Heights
VICTORIAN CHARM AND FUNKY FUN

STABLISHED IN THE 1890S as Houston's first "planned community," the Heights is now home to an eclectic community of young professionals, artists, and musicians. The heart of this near-town neighborhood is Heights Boulevard, a 60-foot-wide, tree-lined thoroughfare and esplanade that was modeled on Boston's Commonwealth Avenue.

The quiet, shady streets of the Heights are perfect for strolling or biking, lined with colorful Victorian-era homes lovingly restored to their original gingerbread splendor. The two of you will delight in discovering cozy cafes and coffeehouses, quaint shops and galleries, and a delightfully vibrant arts scene, ranging from traditional opera to postmodern "art cars."

PRACTICAL NOTES: Time your trip to catch one of the four major Heights community festivals that draw visitors from all over Houston. Try the **Heights Historic Home & Garden Tour** (second week in April) or the **Heights 5K Fun Run and Walk** (first Saturday in June), one of the most entertaining and laid-back outdoor athletic events you'll find in town. The biggest block party in the 'hood is the **Heights Festival** (first Sunday in October), with live music, parades, food, crafts, and about 60,000 other face-painted and costumed urban tourists to celebrate with you. At Christmastime Heights homes festively deck their halls for the **Heights Holiday Open House** (first week in December), complete with carolers and eggnog.

◆ Make yourselves at home in the handsome **Angel Arbor Bed & Breakfast** (848 Heights Boulevard; 713–868–4654 or 800–722–8788).

◆ Dine à deux under the ivy trellises at **Java Java** (911 West Eleventh Street; 713–880–5282), a combination neighborhood cafe and flower shop.

◆ Spend the morning exploring this lovely neighborhood by bike or by blades . . . or just stroll, hand in hand, along the shady boulevards. Then stop by the **Big Time Café** (3700 Washington Avenue; 713–861–3010) for a down-home luncheon of po' boys and potato salad.

◆ Experience some outrageous art—on wheels!—at the **Art Car Museum**, fondly known in the neighborhood as the "Garage Mahal." For an afternoon delight, check out the authentic soda fountain action at the **Yale Grill** (2100 Yale Street; 713–861–3113), and share a malted with two straws.

◆ Dine at the **Cosmos Café** (69 Heights Boulevard; 713–802–2144) and stick around afterward for music that's local and live, or dance the night away at the high-energy **Fabulous Satellite Lounge** (3616 Washington; 713–869–2665) just down the street.

◆ Sleep luxuriously late, then join everybody who's anybody for a friendly morning-after breakfast at the **Eleventh Street Cafe** (748 East Eleventh Street; 713–862–0089) of Texas proportions.

DAY ONE: evening

Take the Heights Boulevard exit north from Interstate 10 to find your romantic hideaway for the weekend, the **Angel Arbor Bed & Breakfast** (848 Heights Boulevard; 713–868–4654 or 800–722–8788; $95 to $125, www.angelarbor.com). The charming hostess of this red-brick Georgian-style inn, Marguerite Swenson, has recently published her own cookbook, so you know you can expect some very special breakfast treats. Swenson has lots of "romantic suggestions" and a map of local antiques stores to share with you.

In the blessedly "un-frilly" main house, each of the upstairs rooms has a private bath and shares a glassed-in porch with views of the garden, its resident stone angel, and the downtown skyline—it's that close. Best bets for romance is the pair of rooms upstairs in the separate carriage house, on the other side of the garden. Both the Michael's Glen room and the Angel's Garden room have whirlpool tubs for two; these two rooms can also be joined into a suite for two couples traveling together. The carriage-house accommodations have separate entrances for complete privacy *and* off-street parking—a lucky break in the narrow streets of the Heights.

DINNER

 Just a few blocks from your inn is **Java Java** (911 West Eleventh Street, 713–880–5282; inexpensive), a quirky little cafe cum flower shop that's open for dinner on weekends only (though breakfast and lunch are on offer seven days a week). The walls are fancifully painted with topiary trees, while branches of artificial ivy twined with tiny twinkling lights festoon the ceiling, creating the magical feel of a secret garden. Try any of the imaginative Tex-Mex specialties and don't overlook the strangely named but delicious concoction known as a "waffelupa." For dessert wrap yourselves around the sinfully rich chocolate cheesecake with a cup of frothy cappuccino.

On your way out of **Java Java,** splurge on an extravagant armload of fragrant crimson roses. Fill a bedside vase back at Angel Arbor, sprinkle a few petals strategically across your pillows, or float handfuls to perfume your whirlpool. Reserve one slender rose to hold between your teeth as a prelude to a seductive tango . . . first removing the thorns, of course.

DAY TWO: morning

BREAKFAST

Start your day in Angel Arbor's sunny dining room and don't be afraid to indulge in the fresh pastries and croissants. (You'll need a hearty base for your morning outdoors, don't you know.) Take your time—take your coffee out to the garden patio, under the kind gaze of the inn's guardian angel.

This morning you'll leave the car in the driveway and explore your new neighborhood in old-fashioned leisure. You can ride your own bicycles or whiz along on roller blades (if you brought them), jog the esplanade path, or just stroll the shady sidewalks. The great advantage of strolling, of course, is the ease of holding hands; but you'd already thought of that.

We suggest you wander north along Heights Boulevard to admire the fanciful "painted ladies": the elaborately restored Victorian homes that are the pride of the Heights. Then turn east along any shaded side street that catches your fancy and enjoy the architecturally diverse mix of Queen Anne and Cajun-influenced cottages and Craftsman-style bungalows. Roam as far afield as you like and don't worry about getting lost: The numbered streets that run east-west get larger as you go north, smaller as you return south (or you can ask the Swensons for a pocket-sized map of the Heights, just in case).

DAY TWO: afternoon

Head back to the inn at the first sign of hunger pangs; by now you should be feeling limber and loose and thoroughly relaxed. (If not, perhaps you two should consider a long, luxurious soak in the whirlpool before lunch?)

LUNCH

Lunch is waiting just a few blocks south on Heights Boulevard at Washington Avenue—yes, you may take your car—at the **Big Time Café** (3700 Washington Avenue; 713–861–3010; inexpensive). Owner and raconteur Keith Coit has combined the best of Texas and Louisiana tradition in this down-home roadhouse, dishing up extraordinary po' boy sandwiches along with family-recipe coleslaw and potato salad. We're particularly fond of his vegetarian Sharecropper sandwich, made with three kinds of squash and cheeses, and a salad bowl's worth of fresh veggies. Besides food Coit is also passionate about hot sauces—he's collected over a hundred varieties—and "boutique" root beers. You two can sprawl lazily on the wooden deck out front or sit side by side at the counter and join in the good-ol'-boy banter between Coit and his customers.

Driving back from lunch, north along Heights Boulevard, keep a sharp eye out for a fantastic, shimmering pile of silvery . . . um, junk? You really can't miss it. Those surreal spikes and spires mark Houston's justly famous **Art Car Museum** (140 Heights Boulevard; 713–861–5526; free), known to its fans as the Garage Mahal. Inside expect the unexpected. Anything with wheels and a motor is a candidate for Art Car stardom, from the turf-sprouting Lawnmobile to the filigreed-iron VW bug to the classic low rider adorned with fangs.

You can spend the afternoon in air-conditioned comfort admiring the cars, the avant-garde videos projected on a wall of TV screens, or chatting with the delightful characters who run this crazy show. You two brought your camera, right? If not, pick out a postcard or two to remember this fantasy world.

Stop by the authentic 1950s-era soda fountain at the nearby **Yale Grill** (2100 Yale Street; 713–861–3113). To get there, follow Heights Boulevard north to Twentieth Street, turn right onto Twentieth, and then right onto Yale Street. Pretend it's your first date in the days of poodle skirts and letter sweaters and lean close together on

Art Cars, Drivin' You Crazy

Some people just can't get enough of Houston's art cars; hence the need for a museum, an annual parade, and the sexiest, hippest party in town: the yearly **Art Car Ball**. The parade and ball coincide with the **Houston International Festival** each April. Anybody with fifty bucks to get in is welcome at this charitable ball, which, unlike its hoity-toity brethren, is way more about cool than couture: Black garb is good; leather is better. The party's held in a downtown parking garage, and once you've plunked down the cash, it's all you can eat and drink. Dance under the stars and the skyline lights all night long or as long as you last. Special staged events at previous balls have included a midnight bullfight (the bull was a VW; the matadors rode mopeds) and a wedding on roller blades. Unplanned exuberant outbursts may be expected.

the twirl-around stools at the counter. Order a malt or a milkshake to share with two straws, and maybe a piece of pie from the glass case. This sweetly old-fashioned cafe used to be a pharmacy; now it's a grill, a gift shop, and a post office—so you can mail those Art Car postcards here!

DAY TWO: evening

Tonight you've got a high-energy agenda of dining and dancing to live music. Don't fret about dress; these neighborhood venues are decidedly casual. Just slip into something black, maybe show a little skin or reveal a wickedly placed tattoo, and you'll blend right in with the urban, twenty-to-thirty-something crowd.

DINNER

Hop in the car and drive back to the intersection of Heights Boulevard and Washington Avenue, though this time you're headed for the **Cosmos Café** (69 Heights Boulevard; 713–802–2144; inexpensive), just north of your lunch date at Big Time. It may look like a wood-paneled den and barroom, but your food-loving hostess, Deanna Rund, has some great Southwestern-style cuisine on her bill of fare. Do start with the luscious goat cheese and pesto terrine; then explore the entrees, fragrant with fresh-grown herbs from Rund's backdoor garden. After dinner stick around: There's live music on weekend nights at the Cosmos, featuring some rockin' local talent. Expect hard-driving R&B, maybe some smoky Texas blues, a little of that irresistible Cajun zydeco . . . you never know.

Like to hear more? Then stroll half a block east on Washington Avenue to the **Fabulous Satellite Lounge** (3616 Washington; 713–869–2665). On weekends the Satellite is crowded, raucous, and a whole lot of fun, featuring a well-selected roster of famous and soon-to-be-famous Austin bands. Forget about finding a seat; you'll be dancing from the minute you get there. For a breather and some make-out room, explore the darker, much quieter patio out back.

DAY THREE: morning

BREAKFAST or BRUNCH

We're betting you'll want to sleep in this morning, so draw the curtains, hide the alarm clock, and savor a leisurely snooze. When you're ready to face the day, there's no better restorative than the old-fashioned breakfast dished up at the **Eleventh Street Cafe** (748 East Eleventh Street; 713–862–0089; inexpensive). This red-brick diner is a neighborhood institution, where you're liable to meet anyone who's anybody in the Heights. Your bartender from last night might be sitting with the stockbroker whose restored home you admired on yesterday's walkabout. Grab a newspaper and a cup of coffee while you consider your options, bearing in mind that biscuits are Texas-big here and eggs are cooked to your heart's desire. Sure, the service here is sometimes slow, but that's all the better for dalliance, bringing your weekend to a sweet, unhurried close.

Heights Highbrow
A Night at the Opera

HERE'S MORE TO THE HEIGHTS music scene to tug at your heart strings. How about an intimate evening with the neighborhood's gem of an opera company? This itinerary guides you two through the finer things in the Heights, including some notably romantic dining escapes.

PRACTICAL NOTES: The highbrow heart of this itinerary is a performance of **Opera in the Heights,** a charming regional company perfect for opera lovers and novices alike. Seats for the five-show season are considerably less expensive than those at Houston's Grand Opera downtown, too, generally only $20 to $25. For program information and tickets, call (713) 861-5303 or check the company's Web site at www.feelthelove.org/oprahts.htm. Make your plans early, as the widespread appeal of Opera in the Heights makes for many a sold-out show.

DAY ONE: evening

This weekend you'll make yourselves at home in the enchanted surroundings of **Sara's Bed & Breakfast Inn** (941 Heights Boulevard; 713-868-1130 or 800-593-1130; $70 to $125). Your hosts, Bob and Connie McCreight, have lovingly restored this Victorian beauty in a pale shade of raspberry with white trim, complete with brick walkways and a wrought-iron fence all around.

The most wonderful settings for storybook romance are Sara's two upstairs suites. The Austin Suite ($125) has its own sitting room and private balcony at the front of the house; its private bath has both a shower and a clawfoot tub. The Tyler Suite ($105) also has a

Romance AT A GLANCE

◆ While away a fairy-tale weekend at **Sara's Bed & Breakfast Inn** (941 Heights Boulevard; 713–868–1130 or 800–593–1130).

◆ Drink in the sunset, the skyline, and salty margaritas on the patio of the **King Biscuit Café** (1606 White Oak Drive; 713–861–2328).

◆ Savor classic French cuisine at **Tour d'Argent** (2011 Ella Boulevard; 713–864–9864), a little log cabin "lost" in the woods.

◆ Browse the gypsy-ish collection of shops along Nineteenth Street for eclectic art, antiques, and fragrant potions, then find a tasty brunch or lunch on the narrow brick terrace of the **Kaldi Café** (250 West Nineteenth Street; 713–802–2246).

◆ Set the stage for romance at a cozy, family-run cafe, **Tutto Bene** (4618 Feagan Street; 713–864–0209), then swoon to love stories on a grand scale at **Opera in the Heights** at the **Lambert Hall Performing & Visual Arts Education Center** (1703 Heights Boulevard; 713–861–7211).

◆ For more amore, drop by **Dacapo's** Italian bakery (1141 East Eleventh Street; 713–869–9141) and breakfast on espresso and croissants at a sunny sidewalk table.

private bath and sitting area, but even better is the winding spiral staircase leading to the third-story widow's walk—you'll have the open air, the treetops, and a stunning view of the downtown skyline all to yourselves.

Drop your bags and try not to linger too long in your love nest, because tonight you'll treat yourselves to a breathtaking sunset vista with a well-chosen cocktail or two.

The friendly, funky little **King Biscuit** (1606 White Oak Drive; 713–861–2328; inexpensive) began its life as a service station, believe it or not, but now it's a cozy cafe boasting an outdoor patio with one of the city's best views of the downtown skyline. Settle yourselves at a secluded table for two and choose a cocktail from the fully stocked bar—we recommend the margaritas made with fresh lime juice. Need a nibble with that? Try a plate of quesadillas made with fresh Mexican cheese and lightly seasoned shredded pork. By the time the sun slides past the horizon, you two should be remembering why you fell in love in the first place.

DINNER

After the all-natural light show is over, you lovers will be ready for a romantic late supper at **La Tour D'Argent** (2011 Ella Boulevard; 713–864–9864; expensive, reservations recommended). You might hold hands like Hansel and Gretel as you approach this rustic lodge in the magical woods, said to be Houston's oldest log cabin. Inside, though, the cuisine is classic French. Begin with lamb-stuffed puff pastry or smoked salmon mousse; then try beef tenderloin Bordelaise or veal medallions richly swathed in morel mushroom sauce.

More Romantic Sunsets

Houston's year-round, mostly mild weather means a number of urban green spaces in which to relax, al fresco, and catch the sunset over the skyline. Two outstanding choices for cocktails as the sun sinks over the yardarm are the second-story wooden deck at **Sonoma** *(1415 California Street; 713–522–7066) or—for an even loftier perspective—the tenth-story terrace at Scott Gertner's* **Skybar** *(3400 Montrose; 713–520–9688), perched atop Montrose's only "sky-scraper." Prefer to pack your own silver shaker of martinis? Then try one of the many "pull-ins" along Allen Parkway in the Bayou Park; we particularly like the Henry Moore sculpture and fountain just east of Waugh Drive.*

DAY TWO: morning

After breakfasting at your inn, you'll spend a leisurely morning browsing the wonderful collection of art and antiques stores lining Nineteenth Street just north of your bed-and-breakfast. If you're feeling energetic, by all means walk the dozen or so blocks; if not, take the car, as you'll find plenty of parking. This 2-block strip of Nineteenth Street is a gypsy-ish assortment of merchants in old-fashioned store-fronts, offering treasures that range from fashionably funky to formally beautiful.

Our favorite stop is the **October Gallery Pavilion** (244 West Nineteenth Street, 713–861–3411), that modestly bills itself as a "National Art Park." Most of the artwork in ceramic, glass, stone, and wood is locally done and one of a kind, so if you see something you can't live without, best buy it. Explore the gallery's selection of fragrant body oils, handmade soaps, and luxury-line incense and candles; you two should plan ahead for a sensuous, scented soak tonight in your clawfoot tub.

We also like **Casa Ramirez Imports,** right across the street (239 West Nineteenth Street; 713–880–2420). The minute you step across the threshold, you're enveloped in the sights and scents of a Mexican market. The folk art on jumbled display here includes Day of the Dead altars and dancing skeletons, brightly colored *loteria* cards, and whimsically carved and painted animals from Oaxaca. Look carefully to find love potions and *milagro* charms amid the saints and devils; you'll surely find what you need to cast an amorous spell over your weekend.

DAY TWO: afternoon

LUNCH

The moment you're feeling peckish, amble back to the blue-awninged entrance of the **Kaldi Café** (250 West Nineteenth Street; 713–802–2246; inexpensive), slotted in next door to the October Gallery Pavilion. Place your orders at the counter and then settle in at one of the sunny tables outdoors on the cafe's narrow, brick-walled terrace. For an eye-opening brunch, get the sultry Belgian waffles flavored with fresh-brewed coffee. Choosing between the seductive soups, salads, and sandwiches for lunch can be a delightful dilemma. We like Kaldi's sophisticated take on a standard ham-and-cheese sandwich, made with goat cheese, roasted tomatoes, and ham dressed with tarragon mayonnaise and piled onto a flaky croissant. If you're truly stumped, try the "half and half" combo as a compromise: two of any half sandwich, half salad, or cup of soup.

After lunch, if you're so inclined, you might visit one or two more stores in the neighborhood. We like **Yubo's** (1012 Yale; 713–862–3239), on Yale between Tenth and Eleventh Streets, for upscale folk art and furnishings; and **Bella Luna** (701 East Eleventh

A Little Taste of Texas

Is opera just too tragic for your taste? Does R&B give you the blues? Well, darlin', don't give up on the Heights music scene before sampling the blue-jeans blend of barbecue and bluegrass at Hickory Hollow (101 Heights Boulevard; 713–869–6300; inexpensive). Chow down on slow-smoked beef brisket or chicken-fried steak—two of the national foods of Texas—then tap your toes to a variety of weekend live-music acts. A well-plucked banjo can set your heartstrings just a-janglin'.

Street; 713–864–8640), just east of Heights Boulevard, for sophisticated furnishings, architectural elements, and even a selection of gourmet coffee beans. Both are conveniently located on the way back to your inn.

Or if it's a pretty afternoon, you might prefer a hand-in-hand stroll along the shady esplanade of Heights Boulevard. Drop off the car at your inn and pick up your camera: The mini-park's quaint, white-painted gazebo makes a perfect setting for a keepsake photograph of the two of you.

DAY TWO: evening

DINNER

To set the operatic mood, soulful Italian food is perfect, so your dinner date tonight is at a cozy, family-run cafe, **Tutto Bene** (4618 Feagan Street; 713–864–0209; moderate, reservations recommended). It's easy to find, only a few blocks south of your inn on Feagan Street between Shepherd and Yale.

Picture yourselves at a secluded, candlelit table for two, sharing a steaming dish of pasta, a good bottle of red wine, and the discreet attentions of an almost-corny accordionist with a repertoire of Mediterranean love songs: That's *amore*, darlings. But don't tarry too long over your Amarettos and cheesecake, as the opera frowns on latecomers. Fortunately, you can zip back up Heights Boulevard in less than ten minutes, stress free.

Love stories on a grand scale await you at tonight's opera, in the intimate setting of the **Lambert Hall Performing & Visual Arts Education Center** (1703 Heights Boulevard; 713–861–7211). Attending the opera in this 325-seat auditorium, formerly a church sanctuary and still bejeweled with stained-glass windows, is like "listening in your living room," as one aficionado remarked.

Not many neighborhoods can boast their own regional opera company, but thanks to the vision and passionate support of Heights music lovers, the company of **Opera in the Heights** thrives. Recent romantic programs have included Verdi's *La Traviata*, Donizetti's *L'Elisir D'Amore*, and—a special treat for opera lovers— Mascagni's *L'Amico Fritz*, which had not been performed in the United States in more than seventy years.

In the hushed darkness of the opera house, the strains of beautiful music will transport you, eliciting sighs and soft, stolen kisses. Afterward, back at your inn, perhaps you can reenact your favorite scenes of doomed lovers or softly sing duets amid the bubbles in your clawfoot bath.

DAY THREE: morning

BREAKFAST

This morning you'll take it slow and easy. Lounge late in bed; then join your fellow guests for breakfast in the cheery dining room at Sara's.

Or if you two wake with arias still dancing in your heads, you might drop by **Dacapo's** Italian bakery (1141 East Eleventh Street; 713–869–9141) for espresso, croissants, and chocolate éclairs. You can drive or walk north on Heights and then turn right onto Eleventh Street for 2 blocks. If the weather's fine, choose one of the sidewalk tables to watch the world go by. After this weekend's operatic heights, you'll want to take time to savor the morning, each other's company, and la dolce vita.

River ☉Oaks

BIG MONEY IN THE OLD SOUTH

HIS WEEKEND ITINERARY IS DEVOTED to the endless seductions of wealth. Just west of Montrose, the palatial homes of River Oaks are jaw-dropping monuments to the theory that more is more, much more. Tara itself, transplanted here, would look like a sharecropper's shack: River Oaks residents include Saudi princes and local potentates. While it's true that money may not buy you love, flirting with the lifestyles of the rich and famous can be very, very sexy.

PRACTICAL NOTES: Houston is famous for its azaleas, which put on a blooming show of red, pink, purple, and white every spring. The most breathtaking display in early March coincides with the **Azalea Trail** tour of River Oaks homes and gardens. It's a truly special time to see River Oaks gardens at their romantic finest and to peek inside fabulous estates not otherwise open to the public. The tour is usually scheduled for the first two weekends in March; for more information call the River Oaks Garden Club at (713) 523–2483.

Both the mansions described in this itinerary are open to the public year-round, not just during the Azalea Trail tour, but you'll want to call in advance to be sure of tour times and to find out about special events. For **Bayou Bend** call (713) 639–7750; the **Rienzi Estate** is open Thursday through Monday (713–639–7800).

DAY ONE: afternoon

From West Loop 610, exit San Felipe and turn east, then turn left on Briar Oaks Lane. The hotel currently known as the **St. Regis** (1919 Briar Oaks Lane; 713–840–7600; $190 to $275 and up) has undergone

44

Romance
AT A GLANCE

◆ Lounge in the lap of luxury at the **St. Regis** (1919 Briar Oaks Lane: 713–840–7600), where you can indulge in a veddy British afternoon tea . . . among other pleasures.

◆ At dinnertime, revel in the English country-house comfort of **Ouisie's Table** (3939 San Felipe at Willowick; 713–528–2264).

◆ Tour fabulous mansions in River Oaks, like the lush **Bayou Bend Collection & Gardens** (enter from 1 Westcott Street or 2940 Lazy Lane; 713–639–7750), and the gorgeous **Rienzi Estate** (1406 Kirby Drive; 713–639–7800), both wings of the Houston Museum of Fine Arts.

◆ Lunch in refined style at **Andre's Tea Room and Swiss Pastry Shop** (2515 River Oaks Boulevard at Westheimer; 713–524–3863), a longtime River Oaks favorite.

◆ Dine in an elegant game lodge worthy of Lady Chatterley at the **Rainbow Lodge** (1 Birdsall Street; 713–861–8666), widely regarded as the most romantic restaurant in Houston.

◆ Breakfast in the company of local moguls at unassuming **Avalon Drug Co. and Diner** (2417 Westheimer Road; 713–527–8900), then shop for high-priced baubles at the **Antique Pavilion** (2311 Westheimer Road; 713–520–9755) next door. If big numbers make you nervous, don't look at the price tags!

◆ Round out your weekend watching a chukka or two of polo in nearby Memorial Park (call the Houston Polo Club for details; 713–622–7300), or stroll the leafy grounds of the **Houston Arboretum and Nature Center** (4501 Woodway; 713–681–8433).

more name changes than Elizabeth Taylor has husbands. But one thing has remained the same—whether you call it the Remington or the Ritz-Carlton or the Sheraton Luxury Collection—and that is pure, unadulterated opulence. This posh spot is one of the most elegant hostelries in town. (Luxury, after all, was one of its middle names.) Here you'll be cosseted and fussed over in grand style; rooms on the Astor Floor even include twenty-four-hour personal butler service.

Although all the tastefully furnished rooms at the St. Regis include downy-soft beds and European-style duvets, marble baths, and fully stocked guest refrigerators, you may prefer a larger suite in which to act out your rich-and-famous fantasy. The executive suites are an excellent choice, with a separated bedroom and living room, wet bar, and whirlpool tub for two. The pinnacle of St.

Regis accommodation is the Presidential Suite, a palatial 2,000 square feet complete with two bedrooms, three baths, two living rooms, and a formal dining room fit for the fanciest dinner party.

Do try to check in early your first afternoon to indulge in the sybaritic ritual of traditional afternoon high tea, held daily from 3:00 to 5:00 P.M. in the plush environs of the Tea Lounge. Nibble at dainty tea sandwiches, tiny pastries, fresh fruits, and thick Devonshire cream; choose from several classic blends of tea or sip French champagne. You two can pose as visiting British royalty while a harpist plucks softly in the background, but please, don't crook your pinkies.

If tea for two isn't quite your style, don your nattiest workout gear instead and take advantage of the exercise gear at the private poolside health club. Or swim a few laps in the beautifully landscaped outdoor pool, "climate controlled" for ultimate comfort. Afterward you can laze side by side in sunny chaise longues, and take turns slathering each other with Bain de Soleil.

DINNER

For dinner tonight you lovebirds will sink deep into the English country-house comfort of **Ouisie's Table** (3939 San Felipe at Willowick; 713–528–2264; moderate to expensive; reservations recommended) which is just a block or two west of your hotel. The elegant fare is Southern deluxe with a pronounced Southwestern accent. If the evening's fine, ask for a candlelit table on the secluded outdoor terrace, its soft-splashing fountain delightfully fringed with aromatic herbs.

We like the blackened Gulf redfish crowned with crabmeat and fresh jumbo shrimp, and the pecan-crusted chicken richly stuffed with Brie, spinach, and wild rice, served with roasted mashed sweet potatoes.

Back at the St. Regis, the clubby environs of the newly refurbished Remington Grill make an ideal backdrop for a proper nightcap. Snuggle into one of the leather loveseats and try a respectably aged port or a nutty-flavored dry sherry. Then toddle off to your room to find the Godiva chocolate waiting on your pillow. Sweet dreams.

DAY TWO: morning

BREAKFAST

This morning pamper yourselves with breakfast in bed, choosing from the amazing selection of St. Regis room-service delicacies. We particularly like the pecanwood-smoked salmon with cream cheese on toasted bagels and the steaming-hot Earl Grey tea in a heavy silver service.

After breakfast you'll start your River Oaks tour with its most famous estate, the former mansion of philanthropist Miss Ima Hogg. (To prevent you any embarrassment later, we'll tell you now that yes, Ima Hogg was really her name, and no, she decidedly did *not* have a sister named Ura. That's purely a fiction of wicked local wags.) Miss Ima, as she's affectionately remembered, donated her family's mansion, its fabulous contents, and surrounding fourteen lushly landscaped acres to Houston's Museum of Fine Arts. Now known as the **Bayou Bend Collection & Gardens** (enter from 1 Westcott Street or 2940 Lazy Lane; 713–639–7750), the palatial estate is the museum's American Decorative Arts wing, a lavish showcase for antique American furniture and art.

At the imposing doorway of the Latin Colonial edifice, turn back to admire the view of terraced lawns, formal gardens, and wild woodland beyond—it's one of Houston's prettiest panoramas. Look for the icy-white marble statue of Diana reflected in the pool at her feet. Once inside, allow yourselves plenty of time to explore the incredible array of furniture, decorative objects, art, and textiles that Miss Ima spent a lifetime collecting; its cataloguing alone took museum staffers a decade.

DAY TWO: afternoon

LUNCH

From Bayou Bend it's only a short drive down River Oaks Boulevard to **Andre's Tea Room and Swiss Pastry Shop** (2515 River Oaks Boulevard at Westheimer; 713–524–3863; moderate). This short but oh-so-imposing street begins at the high iron gates of the River Oaks Country Club—sorry, members only!—and runs straight as a ruler down to the main thoroughfare of Westheimer. Unlike some of the more heavily forested enclaves of River Oaks, the proud mansions of this boulevard are highly visible from the street for your sightseeing pleasure.

Now owned by a charming French couple, Thierry and Danielle Tellier, Andre's is a longtime River Oaks favorite for refined lunches and exquisite pastries. Try the Caesar salad with Thierry's own "secret" dressing recipe and any of the creamy soups; then choose your delectable desserts from the shiny glass cases at the entrance. From golden, flaky apple-raisin croissants to silky dark chocolate-orange mousse to the richly extravagant strawberry-vanilla buttercream cake with kirsch, the Telliers soothe the fiercest sweet-tooth ache.

This afternoon you'll explore another fantasy palace, this one also a wing of the Fine Arts Museum. But whereas Bayou Bend focuses on Americana, the **Rienzi Estate** (1406 Kirby Drive; 713–639–7800) is devoted to European art.

Rienzi is one of those River Oaks homes that cannot be seen from the street: It's not until you round the last bend of the curved driveway that you'll spy this gorgeous little gem. Although designed by the same Houston architect, John Staub, who created Bayou Bend, one-story Rienzi is much smaller, a mere 12,000 square feet situated on four and a half acres of gently sloping gardens and woods. The beguiling net effect is half sixteenth-century Palladian villa, half 1950s Texas ranch house. Allow an hour for the docent-guided tour from ballroom to bedrooms, dominated by an astonishing collection of French and English china; then add some extra time to stroll through the pleasant gardens.

DAY TWO: evening

DINNER

The most suitable grand finale to all this grandeur is dinner at the **Rainbow Lodge** (1 Birdsall Street; 713–861–8666; expensive; www.rainbow-lodge.com), widely regarded as the most romantic restaurant in Houston. At one time the private home of a wealthy doctor, the lodge and its grounds back up to the Bayou Bend estate you toured this morning. As its name suggests, the Rainbow Lodge will remind you of a fantastical hunting lodge, all woodsy pine and cedar polished to a rich, mellow gleam. The zoo's worth of mounted trophy heads and the astonishing Tie Fly Bar, a hand-carved 20-foot-long representation of a lively trout stream, appeal to those who like their outdoor activities rough and tumble; the lovely sloping lawn and pretty gazebo are popular with those who prefer a more pastoral view of nature.

The food is every bit as gorgeous as the setting. From the menu famous for its game dishes, we highly recommend the mixed grill of venison medallion, breast of quail, pheasant sausage, and spring lamb chop; and the spice-rubbed duckling, rotisseried slowly over a pecan-and-oak fire.

When you make your reservations, be sure to ask for Table 34, a very private two-top snuggled into its own bay window, demurely shielded by velvet drapes from the eyes of other diners. As many proposals have been proffered at this table as marriages held on the grounds, staffers say. Between sips, nibbles, and kisses, look out across the moonlit lawn for the family of resident raccoons—gourmets, too, to judge from their girth.

DAY THREE: morning

BREAKFAST

If you can possibly tear yourselves away from the lap of luxury at the St. Regis, it's only a short drive east along Westheimer to the **Avalon Drug Co. and Diner** (2417 Westheimer Road; 713–527–8900). This old-fashioned diner dishes out homey breakfast foods in spades, from poached eggs to fluffy pancakes. Should the brisk ministrations of the often tart-tongued waitresses seem like a jolt after all that bowing and scraping at the St. Regis, comfort yourselves with the knowledge that many of your fellow diners are the same movers and shakers who built River Oaks in the first place.

Afterward step next door to the **Antique Pavilion** (2311 Westheimer Road; 713–520–9755). Should you wish to re-create that big-bucks

River Oaks ambience in your own home, this is the place to shop. Brace yourselves for heart-stopping price tags spiraling into the $25,000 range.

FOR MORE ROMANCE

Round out your royal weekend watching a chukka or two of polo in nearby Memorial Park. Phone the **Houston Polo Club** for schedules and ticket prices at (713) 622–7300.

Sunday is also a soothing time to visit the **Houston Arboretum and Nature Center** (4501 Woodway; 713–681–8433), a sanctuary for native plants and wildlife just north of your hotel. Put on a pair of sensible shoes to traipse over nearly 5 miles of trails and find your own private space in more than 150 acres of forest, pond, and prairie habitats. It's so quiet and peaceful in these urban woods that even the roar of traffic from nearby Loop 610 is muffled.

Montrose
INTIMATE ARTS

OUSTON'S FIRST SUBURB, MONTROSE, is now a thoroughly urbane, eclectic mix of mansions, town homes, and ambitiously designed makeovers. Known for its vivid nightlife and outstanding restaurants, and right next door to downtown, Montrose reminds many visitors of Washington, D.C.'s Georgetown district. Our first Montrose itinerary focuses on art: culinary art as well as the fine-art enclave bequeathed by a philanthropic family.

PRACTICAL NOTES: Since you will be dining at some of the city's hottest restaurants, do call ahead for reservations.

Special times to visit Montrose include the **Westheimer Festival** in April and the **Greek Festival,** held the second weekend in October. The wild-and-woolly Westheimer Festival weekend, held on the neighborhood's main drag, is an urban tribal gathering featuring colorful tattoos, body piercing, and pet python snakes. (The much calmer arts-and-crafts portion of this celebration has moved to midtown, a dozen or so blocks away.) The Greek Festival is held on the grounds of an Eastern Orthodox church and spills over into the surrounding blocks just north of the University of St. Thomas. Every year some 30,000 people gather to dine on souvlaki and baklava, drink retsina, and dance à la Zorba. For more information call (713) 526–5377.

DAY ONE: evening

This weekend you lovebirds will snuggle into the **Robin's Nest Bed & Breakfast Inn** (4104 Greeley Street; 800–622–8343 or 713–528–5821; $79 to $120, www.houstonbnb.com). Dramatically

Romance AT A GLANCE

♦ Nestle into the **Robin's Nest Bed & Breakfast Inn** (4104 Greeley Street; 800–622–8343 or 713–528–5821) for the weekend.

♦ This weekend you'll dine with three of Houston's very best chefs, starting with Mark Cox at **Mark's** (1658 Westheimer; 713–523–3800). Afterward, drop by the stylish **Mo Mong** (1201 Westheimer; 713–524–5664) for a nightcap.

♦ Feast your eyes on the extraordinary—and formerly private—art collection of the de Menil family at the **Menil Collection Museum** (1515 Sul Ross Street; 713–525–9400) and the **Cy Twombly Gallery** (1519 Branard Street; 713–525–9450) just behind it.

♦ Lunch at the charming little **Café Artiste** (1601 West Main Street; 713–528–3704), then artfully while away your afternoon at the **Rothko Chapel** (3900 Yupon; 713–524–9839) and the **Byzantine Chapel Fresco Museum** (4011 Yupon; 713–521–3990).

♦ Fabulous four-star dining is yours this evening, compliments of the genial Ruppe clan at **Tony Ruppe's Fine American Food and Wine** (3939 Montrose; 713–852–0852). Afterward, try local recording artist Scott Gertner's tenth-story **Skybar** (3400 Montrose; 713–520–9688) for a sophisticated cocktail and a breathtaking view of the downtown skyline.

♦ Luxuriate in Sunday brunch on the boulevard: Choose from the serious foodie repast at Monica Pope's **Boulevard Bistrot** (4319 Montrose Boulevard; 713–524–6922) or the see-and-be-seen experience at the **River Café** (3615 Montrose Boulevard; 713–529–0088).

decorated in deep jewel tones of burgundy and forest green, accented with touches of gold leaf, exotic print fabrics, and fanciful faux paint schemes, it's as comfortable as staying at grandma's house—if your grandmother was a glamorous gypsy, that is. Your sophisticated, friendly hostess, Robin Smith, used to be a sort of professional gypsy (in the U.S. Foreign Service) and is a Cordon Bleu cook, so you can imagine how good your breakfasts will be.

There are only three guest rooms in this private urban retreat, all wonderful, but our favorite for romance is Antonio's Room, with its plump, queen-size featherbed and private bath. Second choice would be Cecelia's Room, a lighter shade of French provincial, also with a private bath.

DINNER

Your dinner reservations tonight are among Houston's most sought after, and you'll never look more desirable than under the starry, twinkling lights of the former church that houses **Mark's** (1658 Westheimer, between Mandell and Dunlavy Streets; 713–523–3800; expensive). Plead, if necessary, to dine *à deux* in the handsome new Cloister Room, a serene, semiprivate enclave of only a dozen tables. Then prepare to be teased and tempted by chef Mark Cox's delicacies like medallions of quail with fresh foie gras or carpaccio of Kobe beef. Pay special attention to the succulent entrees hot from the flames of Cox's signature grill, like maple-roasted duck bathed in elephant-heart plums and mangoes or oak-crisped chicken in a sherry morel sauce. For dessert consider a playful indulgence like S'mores, Cox's very adult version, that is, made with Belgian chocolate.

After dinner—warm, wined, and dined—you may want to take a walk on the wild side along Houston's Westheimer Strip; think Times Square or Hollywood and Vine and you'll get the picture. (But don't walk, literally: Driving is much more sensible along this sometimes dicey avenue.) Throngs of tattooed and pierced nightclubbers, cross-dressers, voyeurs, lovers, and other strangers will entertain you as you drive east along Westheimer toward downtown Houston. If you like, stop at the stylish **Mo Mong** (1201 Westheimer; 713–524–5664) for a nightcap, its sleek downstairs bar crowded with sexy, cutting-edge couples. Mo Mong can be difficult to find, which only adds to its secretive allure. Look for the blazing neon sign of Hollywood Videos on the south side of Westheimer and you'll discover this two-story urban hideout right behind it.

DAY TWO: morning

After breakfasting at your inn, slip on a pair of comfortable shoes for a day of amazing art. You'll spend the morning at the **Menil Collection Museum** and its associated **Bookstore,** with time for a stop at the **Cy Twombly Gallery**. Then artfully while away your afternoon at the **Rothko Chapel** and the **Byzantine Chapel Fresco Museum.**

The Menil Collection, widely considered one of the most important private collections of the twentieth century, was formerly the private assemblage of wealthy art patrons John and Dominique de Menil. The Menils arranged to share their 15,000 paintings, sculptures, prints, drawings, photographs, and rare books with the people of Houston, building a series of galleries to house them in a charming Montrose neighborhood. Admission is free to all four of these art venues, which are conveniently located within a 4-block area.

If you brought your own bicycles, it's a lovely ride from your inn to the Menil Collection Museum. You'll head west on Alabama Street, passing the quiet, tree-shaded campus of the University of Thomas and riding through pretty neighborhoods of restored 1920s-era bungalows. From Alabama, go south 1 block on either Mulberry or Mandell and you'll find the long, low **Menil Collection Museum** building on Sul Ross (1515 Sul Ross Street; 713–525–9400), framed in white steel and weathered gray cypress. If you decided to drive, you'll follow the same route and use the museum parking lot entrance on Alabama.

The museum's buildings are surprisingly understated when seen from the outside. Some locals compare them unflatteringly to concrete bunkers or pillboxes. None of the exteriors prepare you for the astonishing richness of the visual feasts inside. Even if you're not a wildly passionate fan of the arts, you'll enjoy seeing the dramatic displays and ingenious uses of natural light and space.

Stop at the front desk to pick up the informative pamphlet on the collection; you'll find it has helpful maps on the back panel, both of the Menil galleries in this building and of the other buildings that make up the collection.

Though the Menil Collection is perhaps best known for its Surrealists, particularly the works of René Magritte, we are fond of its African and Oceanic artifacts. Perhaps it's because these muscular carvings of wood and bone are backed by glass-walled garden atriums thick with palms and ferns.

The quiet corners of the museum are tempting for a tête-à-tête, but remember the soft-soled docents who haunt just about every room—they are so helpful with art questions, but put a bit of a damper on romance. A better place for an embrace is under the spreading branches of the old live oak tree, on the green lawn outside at the corner of Sul Ross and Mulberry.

Exit the museum to the north—the way you came in—and you'll discover the **Menil Collection Bookstore** (1520 Sul Ross Street; 713–521–9148) in a small gray cottage just across Sul Ross Street. This renovated one-story bungalow still has its original creaky wooden floors, and its walls are lined floor to ceiling with bookcases full of surprising and unusual art books. You'll also find fun, funky folk art and jewelry, plus posters, calendars, and postcards for sale.

Exit the museum to the south, and you'll find the **Cy Twombley Gallery** (1519 Branard Street; 713–525–9450) just behind it, across Branard Street. This is a tiny, nine-roomed jewel box of a display space, housing the Twombley's abstract paintings and sculpture. Many canvases are epic, room-sized; but many incorporate textual fragments of a very intimate nature.

Do you imagine that abstract expression is the antithesis of romance? Then you must see Twombley's 1985 series of five paintings known as "Analysis of the Rose as Sentimental Despair." These funny valentines drip with gorgeous rosy reds, pinks, lavenders, and mauves; above each canvas the artist has scrawled crises de coeur: "In drawing and drawing you his pains are delectable his flames are like water." Above another, read: "In his despair he drew the colours from his own heart."

Unlike the Menil Collection docents, the Twombley guards stay firmly put in the gallery's antechamber, so you're likely to have each exhibition room to yourselves. Perhaps hidden security cameras will capture your embraces—does that inflame or abash you?

Next door to the Cy Twombley Gallery are the offices of Houston's **Da Camera** chamber music society (1427 Branard Street; 713–524–7601), which, under the direction of Sarah Rothenberg, creates its own singular, stimulating blend of traditional and postmodern live music: eclectic, playful, intellectually challenging. Stop by Da Camera's cottage for performance tickets, as well as the souvenir coffee mugs and posters that will mark you as music cognoscenti.

DAY TWO: afternoon

LUNCH

 Bicycle or saunter 1 more block south along Mandell to find your lunch spot at the charming little **Café Artiste** (1601

West Main Street; 713–528–3704; inexpensive). This casual bistro, brightly painted in primary colors, has the perfect accent of Parisian *bohème* for your day of art. Take a seat outdoors under a gaily striped umbrella and picture yourselves on the Left Bank.

Brunch favorites include the Cajun-spicy interpretation of eggs Benedict dubbed "eggs Arnold," hearty-grained muffins, and freshly brewed and flavored lattes. Or fortify yourselves with the shrimp or steak po' boys: a colossal serving of sautéed beef or shrimp, bell peppers, and caramelized onions tucked into French bread and thickly topped with melted cheese, accompanied by spicy grilled potatoes.

The remaining two stops on the Menil circuit are just a block past the main museum and on the way back to your inn. Cycle or stroll back up to Branard Street and turn east; then turn north on Yupon Street to find the **Rothko Chapel** (3900 Yupon; 713–524–9839). The octagonal chapel—another austere pillbox—was built to house the massive, brooding canvases of abstractionist Mark Rothko, rendered in deep purples ranging to velvety blacks. This chapel was the first of the Menil galleries to open in 1971 and has drawn visitors from all over the world. Art lovers on layover at Houston's Bush Intercontinental Airport (some 40 miles to the north) have been known to hire a taxicab down to Montrose and back again, just to get a glimpse of these Rothko panels.

The guest book is also international at the **Byzantine Chapel Fresco Museum** (4011 Yupon; 713–521–3990), 1 block south on Yupon. You'll find exclamations of appreciation written in Greek, French, Chinese, Spanish, and Italian from visitors to this combination of museum and consecrated space, which also houses Greek Orthodox services of worship. The thirteenth-century fresco fragments, romantically ransomed from thieves and painstakingly restored by the Menil Foundation, are astonishingly mounted and lit within an ethereal framework of freestanding walls of sandblasted glass that hauntingly suggest the shape of the original votive chapel in Cyprus.

With your spirits thus lifted by contemplation of the sublime, retrace this morning's path to your snug accommodations back at the Robin's Nest. You'll have time for a nap—and perhaps a little affectionate dalliance—before slipping into something comfortably sexy for dinner.

DAY TWO: evening

DINNER

Tonight you'll dine with one of Houston's most respected chefs, beloved almost as much for his genial hospitality as his cuisine, at **Tony Ruppe's Fine American Food and Wine** (3939 Montrose; 713–852–0852; expensive). Tony Ruppe—his name rhymes with "loop"—presides over a relaxing space on Montrose Boulevard colored with warm vineyard tints of gold, green, and plum. The whole Ruppe clan—Tony, wife Kathy, and sons Shawn and Nick—treats guests like family, dishing up creative "New American" cuisine with grace and good humor. Offerings include gems like silky-smooth American foie gras seared and served with a spicy, clove-scented pear chutney and pomegranate molasses; a gorgeous veal chop encrusted with black olives and spices; and a standout "bread pudding" stuffing rich with wild mushrooms and walnuts.

When you call for reservations, ask for a table for two in the balcony dining area. This very private upstairs space lends itself well to romantic intrigue; plus it provides a voyeuristic, bird's eye view of your fellow diners below.

After dinner stop by local recording artist Scott Gertner's tenth-story **Skybar** (3400 Montrose; 713–520–9688) for a sophisticated cocktail, a breathtaking view of the downtown skyline, and some very cool jazz. Lovers like you, nuzzling sweet nothings in the moonlight, populate the spacious outdoor terrace; indoors, passionate fans of Gertner's own smooth brand of R&B pack the dance floor every weekend night.

DAY THREE: morning

BRUNCH

This morning we suggest you skip breakfast at your inn, however reluctantly, in favor of one of the two best Sunday-brunch spreads in the city, both with picturesque sidewalk cafe tables and both conveniently close to your inn, just north on Montrose Boulevard.

The Sunday edition of the *New York Times* is well-suited to the intellectual bent of the serious foodie repast at Monica Pope's **Boulevard Bistrot** (4319 Montrose Boulevard; 713–524–6922; moderate). Choose your brunch a la carte from Pope's eclectic menu or the blackboard of daily specials; specialties of the house include imaginative omelets and absolutely anything from the in-house bakery.

Or tote the *Houston Chronicle* to the **River Café** (3615 Montrose Boulevard; 713–529–0088; moderate) for a simpler, see-and-be-seen experience set to the agreeable strains of light jazz. Vibraphonist Harry Sheppard plays every Sunday. Crowd-pleasing brunch entrees include eggs St. Charles, shrimp crepes, or a decadent, sugar-powdered take on French toast.

North Montrose

HIP AND HUMOROUS

*T*HE NORTHERN HALF OF MONTROSE offers an agreeable mix of outdoorsy pursuits in Buffalo Bayou Park and urban pastimes like the funky-but-upscale shopping at the Art Deco River Oaks Shopping Center. This itinerary is set indoors and out, flirtatiously blending cinema, comedy, and canoeing with the twin tonics of fresh air and laughter.

PRACTICAL NOTES: Before you book your weekend, check to see who's playing at the **Laff Stop** (1952-A West Gray; 713–524–2333; www.laffstop.com). Remember, the better known the performer, the sooner you should buy tickets! And bear in mind that twice a year the northern boundary of Montrose, scenic Allen Parkway, transforms into a major parade route: for the Houston Livestock Show and Rodeo Parade in February and for the Art Car Parade during the Houston International Festival in mid-April. Make your inn or hotel reservations far enough in advance for a cat-bird's seat at either celebration.

DAY ONE: evening

This weekend you'll roost in the historic home of a former Houston mayor, now the **Lovett Inn** (501 Lovett Boulevard; 800–779–5224 or 713–522–5224; $105 to $175; www.lovettinn.com), which is located just east of Montrose Boulevard and south of Westheimer. Accommodations are available within the handsome stone house, in the carriage house beyond the formal garden and swimming pool, or in a pair of town houses tucked away just behind the property on a quiet side street.

$\mathcal{R}$omance
AT A GLANCE

♦ A handsome house is your home at **The Lovett Inn Bed & Breakfast** (501 Lovett Boulevard; 800–779–5224; www.lovettinn.com).

♦ Test a tried-and-true formula for romance with dinner at Claire Smith's **Daily Review Café** (3412 West Lamar; 713–520–9217) and a movie at the twelve-screen **River Oaks Plaza Cinema** (1450 West Gray; 713–524–8781) or the baroque **Landmark River Oaks Theatre** (2009 West Gray; 713–524–2175). Afterward, work up some body heat in the made-for-making-out room at **Marfreless** cocktail lounge (2006 Peden; 713–528–0083).

♦ Play on blades or bikes in **Buffalo Bayou Park** and picnic on the grass with a lunch deliciously supplied by **Paulie's** urban deli (1834 Westheimer; 713–807–7271). Then stroll and shop for treasures and trinkets along the palm-lined boulevard of the **River Oaks Shopping Center (**West Gray between Waugh and Shepherd).

♦ Chortle your way through a live comedy show at the **Laff Stop** (1952-A West Gray; 713–524–2333), where nationally known comics, as well as local up-and-comers, take center stage. Before or after the show, dine at the nervy, hip **Urbana** (3407 Montrose; 713–521–1086).

♦ Revel in a sunny Tex-Mex brunch buffet at **Café Noche** (2409 Montrose; 713–529–2409), then paddle your own canoe down the gentle waters of Buffalo Bayou. Arrange your romantic regatta in advance with a small group of like-minded outdoor enthusiasts through **Leisure Learning Unlimited** (www.llu.com; 713–529–4414).

We like the charming Delft-blue and white interior of the Honeymoon Cottage, located upstairs in the carriage house, with its generous balcony and whirlpool tub for two. We also are fond of the sleek upstairs town house, Suite #8. Very quiet and private, it's a perfect city pied-à-terre. Both units boast all the comforts of home, including a small guest refrigerator, a wet bar, and a microwave oven for midnight snacks.

DINNER

This evening you'll join well-known Houston chef Claire Smith for an intimate dinner at her very hip, very tongue-in-cheek **Daily Review Café** (3412 West Lamar; 713–520–9217; moderate; reservations recommended). Back in 1999, you see, Smith won "super chef" status in a starring role on Turner Broadcasting System's *Dinner & a Movie* national cablecast. She cooked up a menu to accompany the to-sigh-for movie *Ghost*, coincidentally starring Houston's hometown heartthrob Patrick Swayze. For that memorable meal Smith dreamed up Steamy Clay Pot Chicken and To-Kill-For Embezzler's Purses. On any given day you're sure to find something delightful on Smith's constantly changing menu. Look for recurring favorites like the baked goat cheese salad or the definitely-not-your-mom's chicken potpie with béchamel cream sauce.

The concrete-floored dining room at the Daily Review is loud, and convivial, and a great deal of fun. If you'd like a wee bit more distance between your table and your neighbor's, however, ask for more private seating on the semienclosed patio overlooking the herb garden.

After dinner you'll revive the classic date formula by slipping into the soothing cool darkness of a movie theater. Pick a hearts-and-flowers first run flick at the twelve-screen **River Oaks Plaza Cinema** (1450 West Gray at Waugh Drive; 713–524–8781) or exercise both intellect and libido at an artsy independent or foreign film at the **Landmark River Oaks Theatre** (2009 West Gray; 713–524–2175). The like-new Plaza offers plush seat comfort, cleanliness, and mix-and-match candies in bulk, begging to be bagged; the intimate Landmark, more than half a century old, boasts restored baroque grandeur and gourmet coffees at the snack counter.

Or you can re-create the scene of the crime, so to speak, by renting *Ghost*, surely one of the most romantic movies ever made, at the nearby **Blockbuster Video** (1917 West Gray; 713–520–0301). Take the video back to your inn . . . switch on the VCR . . . cuddle up in your king-size bed . . . and don't forget the tissues for a good cry.

If you're in the mood for more romance after the movie, we'll let you in on a sexy little secret. Just around the corner from the Landmark River Oaks Theater is one of Houston's landmark clandestine watering holes: the famed—or is it infamous?—**Marfreless** (2006 Peden at McDuffy; 713–528–0083). This secluded sanctuary, which was designed with making out in mind, is hidden away behind an unmarked blue door. (Turn right coming out of the theater and then turn right again on McDuffy. Now look carefully under

the metal staircase, next door to the bridal salon called I Do, I Do.)
Choose a softly lit table for two downstairs or sneak upstairs to find
soft couches and near-Stygian darkness just right for necking.

DAY TWO: morning

Breakfast light and early at your inn this morning; then put on
your most fetching jog togs. You're going to spend the morning
showing off your buff physiques at the park. You two might jog,
skate, or bike along the paved paths of well-manicured **Buffalo
Bayou Park** (along Allen Parkway, between Shepherd Drive and
downtown; 713–845–1000). Or if poetry is more your speed, pack a
paperback edition of Elizabeth Barrett Browning's love sonnets.

On your way to the park, stop by **Paulie's** postmodern deli
(1834 Westheimer; 713–807–7271; inexpensive) to pick up
the makings of the perfect picnic lunch. We're particularly fond of
their grilled shrimp BLT, the olive-laden new-potato salad, and the
colorful Mediterranean pasta salad tossed with artichoke hearts. Be
sure to leave room in your basket for a pair of chocolate-dipped
peanut butter cookies.

Park your car in one of the many turnouts along the westbound
lanes of Allen Parkway, then set off to work up a healthy glow.

The Allen Parkway Hike and Bike Trail follows the serpentine
curves of Buffalo Bayou between downtown and River Oaks; you'll
find the green slopes of Buffalo Bayou Park delightfully un-crowded
and dotted with public art, strikingly well-designed fountains and
sculptures. We're especially fond of the fountain that resembles a
gone-to-seed dandelion, just east of Waugh Drive; it's a great place
to toss in a coin and wish for luck in love. Farther east, toward
downtown, a grassy field separates the curvaceous Henry Moore
sculpture from the Maya-like granite pyramid of the Houston police
memorial, designed by Texas-born artist Jesus Bautista Moroles.

DAY TWO: afternoon

LUNCH

Toward noontime seek out a secluded, shady spot to spread your
blanket, preferably with a panoramic view of the downtown skyline.

Unpack your lunch basket and feast. Afterward—if you brought your Browning—take turns reading verse aloud; lazily count the clouds that pass overhead; pluck petals from daisies to find out who loves whom … as if you didn't know already.

After your picnic in paradise, return to your inn for a hot shower—together, of course—followed, perhaps, by a steamy soak in the whirlpool for two.

This afternoon you'll wander the chi-chi shops of the **River Oaks Shopping Center,** the pretty, palm-tree-lined stretch of West Gray between Waugh and Shepherd known for its authentic 1930s Art Deco decor. Don't-miss destinations include the tongue-in-cheek *objet d'art* collection at **Circa Now Gallery** (1983 West Gray; 713–529–8234), the high-tech approach to roughing it at **Wilderness Equipment** (1977 West Gray; 713–522–4453), and the all-cotton clothing for fashion plates of both sexes at **Cotton Club** (1956 West Gray; 713–522–9101) and **Chico's** (2022 West Gray; 713–524–4787).

DAY TWO: evening

For tonight's entertainment you'll enjoy an evening of laughter at a premiere comedy club. Houston is home to a live-and-kicking comedy circuit whose centerpiece club is in north Montrose: The **Laff Stop** (1952-A West Gray; 713–524–2333; www.laffstop.com; prices vary by performer) hosts nationally known comics as well as local up-and-comers. Paula Poundstone has played here; you might see Harland Williams *(There's Something About Mary)*, Dave Chapelle *(The Nutty Professor)*, or Joe Rogan *(NewsRadio)*. Choose from the eight o'clock show—which is nonsmoking on Saturdays—and then dine fashionably late. Or go to dinner first—life is uncertain!—and then hit the late show starting at 10:30 P.M.

DINNER

Your dinner tonight, whether early or late, will be at **Urbana** (3407 Montrose; 713–521–1086; moderate to expensive), as hip, intelligent, and slightly frenetic as its nervy urban melange of a neighborhood. From its submarine blue-glass mosaics to the frisky soundtrack from the triple TVed bar, it's a rollicking, often raucous feasting place for the Montrose tribes. So much the better that the food, and the service, are both so very good. Recent favorites include gargantuan entree salads bearing generous portions of pecan-grilled salmon, blackened chicken breast, or sesame-seeded yellowfin tuna; wild mushroom quesadillas punched up with roasted poblanos and jalapeños, sweetened with caramelized onions and mango; and a fanciful meatloaf of grilled buffalo with cascabel chili ketchup. We like the deeply upholstered booths between the bar and the dining room, which offer a bird's-eye perspective of both rooms and the beautiful people that fill them. Tonight you can eavesdrop on the titillating trysts of other lovers or stage a steamy show of your own.

DAY THREE: morning

BREAKFAST

After yesterday's exertions, darlings, sleep as late as you like. Brew a pot of coffee at your inn and then laze over the Sunday paper delivered to your door. When you finally do feel like facing the day, head out to the Mexican-influenced Sunday brunch at **Café Noche** (2409 Montrose; 713–529–2409; moderate). We like the umbrellaed tables on the sunny patio, grouped around a fountain, though seated indoors you'll be closer to the buffet spread and farther from the traffic noise of the busy boulevard. Nosh on cooked-to-order huevos and chorizo sausage, home-style pastries, and fresh fruit with cream and sip from tall frosty glasses of fresh, rosy-red watermelon juice. We'll leave it to the two of you to decide whether to bring your urban escape to a gentle landlubber's close here over good food and drink, or to sally forth to test more urban waters.

FOR MORE ROMANCE

If you have time for one last weekend adventure, make it a gentle canoe trip down the sun-dappled (and usually lazy) stream of Buffalo Bayou. An astonishing world of natural greenery will surround you as you drift through Memorial Park, River Oaks, and Bayou Park, the scene of yesterday's delightful dalliance. Along the banks of the bayou you'll find plenty of secluded pools and tree-shaded eddies, perfect for slow kisses and sweet words. Arrange your romantic regatta in advance with a small group of like-minded outdoor enthusiasts through Leisure Learning Unlimited (www.llu.com; 713–529–4414). The afternoon-long tours, professionally guided by a knowledgeable local boatman, cost about $30 per person, including a paddling tutorial, canoes, safety gear, and snacks.

More Montrose

Its Theatrical Charms

ANOTHER WAY OF LOOKING AT MONTROSE is through the thespian lens. This near-town neighborhood boasts the only Equity repertory theater group outside of downtown's major Theater District. Add an opulent hotel suite and a fine bill of fare to the mix, and you've got a soothing, sybaritic weekend getaway.

PRACTICAL NOTES: Plan your theatrical weekend around what's playing at **Stages Repertory Theatre** (3201 Allen Parkway, near Waugh Drive; 713–527–8243; www.stagestheatre.com), and aim for an opening night, if possible.

Committed theater lovers will want to schedule this itinerary to coincide with the annual Stages Southwest Festival of New Plays, held in June. The festival features readings and panel discussions of a broad selection of the country's best new plays, all free to the public. Stages also offers workshop readings of developing plays throughout the year, in partnership with the Edward Albee New Playwrights Workshop of the University of Houston's School of Theatre.

DAY ONE: evening

This weekend you lovebirds will be ensconced in the same luxury that in the past cradled crowned heads of Europe at **La Colombe d'Or Hotel** (3410 Montrose; 713–524–7999; $195–$595), formerly the fabulous Fondren mansion. (Before the Great War, Edward VII and Tsar Nicholas were both on oilman Walter Fondren's guest list.) Each of the five art-and-antiques-furnished rooms at this exquisite

♦ Stay at Houston's most intimate luxury hotel, the Euro-style gem called **La Colombe d'Or** (3410 Montrose; 713–524–7999). Orchestrate a Romanoff-style rendezvous with dinner served in your own private dining room, topped off with vintage port.

♦ Drop some dough in the upscale shops of the **River Oaks Center** (West Gray between Waugh and Shepherd). Discover the delights of a Saturday brunch al fresco at the **Backstreet Café** (1103 South Shepherd; 713–521–2239).

♦ Stop by the piano bar at **Darby's on the Parkway** (3322 D'Amico; 713–522–5305) for a little night music on your way to an off-Broadway hit show at **Stages Repertory Theatre** (3201 Allen Parkway; 713–527–8243; www.stagestheatre.com). Afterward dine fashionably late by candlelight at **La Mora Cucina Toscana** (912 Lovett; 713–522–7412).

♦ Brunch on the boulevard, serenaded by a jazz vibraphonist at the **River Café** (3615 Montrose Boulevard; 713–529–0088). Then schmooze with the actors and directors from last night's **Stages** production in an intimate chat session.

European-style hotel is actually a suite with its own private dining room, mind you; plus there's a magnificent penthouse suite with a marble bath and Jacuzzi. On the ground floor you'll find an excellent restaurant and a mahogany-paneled bar, where fifteen varieties of vintage port are served.

DINNER

Dress to the nines this evening for an elegant supper at your inn. You could, of course, join your fellow guests downstairs in the formal dining room. Play at Duke and Duchess and make a grand entrance descending the staircase. Or, even more enchanting, request a private repast served in the dining room of your own suite, a real Romanoff-style rendezvous.

Dabble with the Colombe d'Or's lavish (and expensive) menu to design an appropriately imperial feast for you and your true love. Start with a toast to the ghost of the doomed tsar—and each other—with icy vodka and follow with homemade blinis topped with fresh Russian Beluga caviar. Then sup on delicately roasted whole baby pheasant or rack of lamb richly encrusted with black olives. Dessert? We recom-

mend the chocolate Marquis, decadently perfumed with Grand
Marnier, or the Parisian-accented crème brûlée "a la cassonnade."

Afterward adjourn to his-and-her leather armchairs in the Colombe
d'Or bar for port, cognac, or Armagnac, choosing from more than
two dozen noteworthy vintages. (If you abstained from dessert earlier, a sophisticated terrine of Roquefort with plump, cognac-
marinated plums and roasted pecans would do nicely for nibbling
now.) Better yet, have this elegant nightcap brought to your suite.
Quietly lock the door and blow out all the candles but one . . .

DAY TWO: morning

This morning you'll wake to fragrant hot coffee and fresh, flaky
croissants. Snuggle into the hotel's thick terry-cloth robes and
lounge to your hearts' content. Afterward you'll saunter along West
Gray between Waugh and Shepherd Drive for some luxury shopping
in the **River Oaks Center.** It's only a few blocks north of your hotel,
but do take the car, the better to bring home all those irresistible
purchases.

Follow our browsing suggestions outlined in the previous itinerary or check out the cloud-soft cotton cashmeres at **Joan Vass
Boutique** (1984 West Gray; 713-522-5520) or the orgiastic gathering of 14,000 gourmet gadgets at **Sur La Table** (1996 West Gray;
713-533-0400). And did you two leave your pampered pooch
home alone? Take the puppy a gourmet treat from **Three Dog
Bakery** (1963-B West Gray; 713-522-7712), which, as far as we
know, is the only bakery in town dedicated to doggies. If you behave
very well, perhaps they'll treat you humans to a glass of wine.

DAY TWO: afternoon

LUNCH

So often a civilized brunch is hard to find on a Saturday, but we've
found an all-weekend-long version for you at the **Backstreet Café**
(1103 South Shepherd; 713-521-2239; moderate), just around the

The Couple
That Cooks Together

*The surest way to your lover's heart is through the stomach; it's true. Spend a steamy hour or two concocting delicacies to delight your sweet one's eye and tongue in a cooking class, like those conducted at **Sur La Table** (1996 West Gray; 713–533–0400) by professional chefs and cookbook authors. Recent courses have embroidered on heartfelt culinary themes like Decadent Chocolate Desserts and Comfort Foods under Cover. More cooking classes and demonstrations can be found nearby at **Williams-Sonoma** (4076 Westheimer, in Highland Village; 713–622–4161); **La Bella Cucina** (1642 Arlington, in the Heights; 713–880–2166); and **Le Panier Cooking School** (7275 Brompton, south of West University; 713–664–9848).*

corner from your happy hunting, er, shopping, grounds. From West Gray turn north on McDuffie Street, and within 2 blocks you'll find the renovated house and pleasant brick patio that's home to the aptly named Backstreet. The good news starts as soon as you are seated with a basket of fresh-baked bread; order an eye-opening mimosa or Bloody Mary to sip while you contemplate the menu. Choose from a variety of well-made sandwiches, like the lobster with red pepper remoulade; inventive salads, like the uptown spin on fried green tomatoes; or just go brunch-y with French brioche toast.

After lunch you'll want to wrap up your shopping and then retreat to your gilded suite at the Colombe d'Or. Chambers this beautiful are worth enjoying at length. An afternoon dalliance and king-size nap might be your prescription for relaxation; certainly, you'll need the rest before this evening's theatrical performances.

DAY TWO: evening

Refreshed and renewed, you'll enjoy another elegant engagement this evening. Head out in your car and start with a preshow cocktail in the intimate environs of the piano bar at **Darby's on the Parkway** (3322 D'Amico; 713–522–5305). Ask pianist Danny Low to play "your" song, or enjoy other sentimental favorites like "Someone to Watch over Me" . . . and don't be too shy to sing along.

The Stages curtain goes up promptly at eight on weekend nights, so you'll be glad to learn that the theater is only a one-block drive away on Allen Parkway. **Stages Repertory Theatre** (3201 Allen Parkway, near Waugh Drive; 713–527–8243; www.stagestheatre.com; $26 to $46) is Houston's only professional Equity company outside the downtown Theater District, and it offers two intimately mid-sized venues: the Arena Stage, which seats 230 patrons, and the Thrust Stage, which seats 175. Recent romantic productions have included the irony-tinged musical *I Love You, You're Perfect, Now Change!* and *Shakespeare's R & J*, a riff on you know who's ever-loving couple—this show, though, is all male.

DINNER

After the theater we recommend **La Mora Cucina Toscana** (912 Lovett; 713–522–7412; moderate to expensive) for a quiet candlelit supper just a few blocks from your hotel. Owner Lynette Mandola's gorgeous Tuscan-inspired dishes are as much admired by other local chefs as by her devoted clientele. You'll fall in love, we predict, with her veal cuchinetti, "pillows" of tender veal stuffed with mozzarella, salty prosciutto, and a garlicky, fresh tomato marinara, gently grilled and topped with herbed white-wine butter sauce. Her unique "spaghetti in a bag," an oven-infused combination of pasta, fresh seafood, and spicy tomato sauce piled into parchment paper, releases a wondrous aroma when slit open at your table. Warm, terra-cotta walls and flattering soft light from the fireplace or the stars above the skylit atrium make this intimate restaurant one of Houston's most romantic spots.

DAY THREE: morning

BRUNCH

Sleep late this morning, if you like; then stroll arm-in-arm the 2 blocks south along Montrose Boulevard to the **River Café** (3615 Montrose Boulevard; 713–529–0088; moderate) for a see-and-be-seen brunch experience set to the agreeable strains of light jazz:

Vibraphonist Harry Sheppard plays every Sunday. (The vibraphone is a sort of kissing cousin of the marimba and the xylophone, in case you were wondering.) Crowd-pleasing a la carte entrees include eggs St. Charles, shrimp crepes, and a decadent, sugar-powdered take on French toast. On pretty mornings regulars vie for the sidewalk tables; to get yours, arrive early or phone in an advance reservation.

FOR MORE ROMANCE

Stick around Sunday evening for Stages's Talk Back Sunday event, which starts "around 5-ish" after the afternoon matinee. Scheduled for the first Sunday of every Stages production, this freeform question-and-answer session allows theater patrons to chat informally with actors, directors, and designers. For theater lovers it's an intimate glimpse behind the scenes not to be missed. There's nothing like schmoozing with the stars to put a sparkle in your lover's eyes; the two of you may be inspired to stage your own private production of Romeo and Juliet afterward. . . .

Art and Nature in the Museum District

OUSTON'S MUSEUM DISTRICT will remind you of Paris, with its wide, tree-lined boulevards, plazas punctuated by fountains and sculptures, and its population of museums and art venues of all shapes and sizes. The heart of this handsome neighborhood is the **Warwick Hotel,** which the globe-trotting comedian Bob Hope once praised as a personal favorite for its stunning views over the Mecom Fountain and the vast expanse of green space that is Hermann Park.

Within easy walking distance of the Warwick, you'll find three major museums, a planetarium, a zoo, an IMAX theater, a sculpture garden, a municipal golf course, and an outdoor amphitheater hosting world-class musical and theatrical productions free to the lucky public. You could spend weeks exploring this neighborhood and still not exhaust the endless opportunities for entertainment and enlightenment.

PRACTICAL NOTES: A production at **Miller Outdoor Theater** in Hermann Park makes an especially memorable keynote for this itinerary. The Miller program runs with the seasonable weather from May through October. Annual highlights include the Juneteenth Celebration, with gospel, blues, and jazz; the Fourth of July festivities, featuring the Houston Symphony's rousing rendition of the "1812 Overture," complete with fireworks and real cannon; and the Shakespeare Festival in August.

To get a schedule of Miller performances, check the theater's Web site at www.ci.houston.tx.us/departme/parks/millerschedule.htm or

Romance AT A GLANCE

◆ Sip art-themed martinis at a happy hour sponsored by the **Contemporary Arts Museum** (5216 Montrose; 713–284–8250; www.camh.org), then check into the opulently restored **Warwick Hotel** (570 Main Street; 713–526–1991).

◆ Dine in Southwest style at the **Sierra Grill** (4704 Montrose; 713–942–7757); then swing into an evening of "all that jazz" at a cozy neighborhood cabaret, **Cezanne** (4100 Montrose; 713–529–1199).

◆ Explore the arts and sciences in the **Museum District**: Houston's **Museum of Fine Arts** (1001 Bissonnet; 713–639–7300; www.mfah.org) and its much-praised **Cullen Sculpture Garden;** and the wildly unconventional **Contemporary Arts Museum** (5216 Montrose; 713–284–8250; www.camh.org).

◆ Take a lunchtime load off at the Warwick's **The Terrace on Main** and then plunge into the Houston **Museum of Natural Science** (One Hermann Circle Drive; 713–639–4600), complete with IMAX, Cockrell Butterfly Center, and McGovern Hall of the Americas.

◆ Pack an elegant picnic at **Butera's Fine Foods & Deli** (4621 Montrose; 713–528–3737); then thrill to a starlit performance—music, dance, or spoken word—at **Miller Outdoor Theater** (Hermann Park, 100 Concert Drive; 713–284–8350).

◆ Enjoy the champagne brunch at the Warwick before spending the afternoon playing in **Hermann Park.** It's all happening at the **Houston Zoological Gardens,** or choose golf or horseback riding for your perfect day in the sun.

send a self-addressed, stamped envelope to Miller Outdoor Theater, 100 Concert Drive, Houston, TX 77030. And be sure to pack a picnic basket and a blanket for your evening under the stars.

DAY ONE: afternoon

Before checking into your hotel, kick off your art-filled discovery weekend with a visual sort of happy hour at the **Contemporary Arts Museum** (5216 Montrose; 713–284–8250; www.camh.org). On the last Friday of every month, the CAM hosts a hip gathering dubbed the Steel Lounge. Starting at 5:30 P.M., you'll mingle with a fashionably black-garbed crowd and sneak-preview the installations and shop for funky gifts, all the while sipping a martini thematically

matched to the current exhibition (like the White Lightning concoction that honored James Turrell's light projections or the Blue
Steel-tini served for Dewitt Godfrey's steel sculpture).

DAY ONE: evening

The **Warwick Hotel** (5701 Main Street; 713–526–1991; $179 to $254)
boasts an astonishing guest list of American presidents (Johnson,
Nixon, Ford, Carter, Bush), dukes and duchesses, princes and
princesses, kings and queens (England, Japan, Belgium, Monaco,
Jordan, Spain), and luminaries ranging from Helen Hayes and
Frank Sinatra to Andy Warhol and Aristotle Onassis. Houston's oldest hotel first opened its elegant doors in 1925 and has recently
undergone a multimillion-dollar face-lift that restored the exterior
to its signature rich terracotta color and the interior to its original
marble-and-gilt glory.

The Warwick's Spirit of Romance package ($210 per night)—
which includes your own parlor suite with king-size bed, champagne and strawberries, and breakfast each morning for two—is
especially attractive. Choose from a sweeping view of Hermann Park
on the west side of the hotel or the panorama of the downtown skyline from the east side.

After check-in, check out the outdoor pool deck on the second floor. You lovebirds will luxuriate in the ambience of a posh
resort. Twenty-foot palm trees line the perimeter, attentive waiters bear icy drinks, and classical statuary poses here and there.
The azure-tiled pool is refreshing in summer and heated in winter, which adds up to year-round indulgence, as far as we're con-
cerned.

DINNER

Dinner this evening is just a few blocks north of the Warwick and
the CAM at the **Sierra Grill** (4704 Montrose; 713–942–7757; moderate to expensive). Sierra is a kicked-back urban retreat, you'll find,
where you'll feel just as comfortable in "good" jeans and artsy acces-
sories as in dressier duds. You'll enjoy picking and choosing from
chef/owner Charlie Watkins's wild, wild Southwest menu. Try the
venison carpaccio, "campfire" salmon, wild-boar enchiladas, or the

fork-tender Sierra Grande, a fifteen-ounce beef tenderloin cooked to your command.

After dinner you'll drive a bit farther north on Montrose to find **Cezanne** (4100 Montrose; 713–529–1199), an intimate jazz venue tucked away up the stairs from the **Black Labrador** English pub. Call ahead to find out what musical treat's in store for you. This unlikely little room hosts some of the best live jazz sets in town from local talent and national tours, ranging from sultry torch singers to sexy sax ensembles. The seating is couch-cushy, dimly lit, and huggably close; too bad the parking is equally tight. Try for a slot in the often-overlooked parking lot in back or scout a spot on the surrounding side streets.

DAY TWO: morning

Take it easy this morning with breakfast in bed, compliments of the Warwick, complete with a sweet-scented rose on your tray. Then put on your art-appreciation shoes for a morning of museum-hopping. Your first stop will be Houston's **Museum of Fine Arts** (1001 Bissonnet; 713–639–7300; www.mfah.org), directly across the street from the Warwick; it houses intriguing permanent collections of African gold and Impressionist paintings, as well as hosting blockbuster traveling exhibits, like the recent controversial display of the Romanoff jewels.

You can wander the MFA's cool, high-ceilinged halls on your own or take a "postcard tour," an unpretentious, self-guided excursion through the galleries. This tour is designed for children but is great fun for grown-ups, too. Follow the instructions on the pack of cards you're given, chock-full of factoids about the art of Africa, Asia, and Europe. Drool over the gorgeous gowns by Worth and Balenciaga in the Textile and Costume Institute; marvel at the African crowns and swords fashioned from solid gold.

Just across Binz Street from the main MFA entrance, you'll find its much-praised **Cullen Sculpture Garden,** a high-walled outdoor sanctuary hushed and leafy with native Texas trees and plants. Wander hand in hand amid the acre of masterworks by twentieth-century giants like Giacometti, Stella, and Shapiro. Secluded benches beckon you for quiet conversation and a heartfelt clinch.

The sculpture garden's green space provides a respite, sort of a psychological breather, between the more formal, traditional collection of the MFA and the wildly unconventional installations at the **Contemporary Arts Museum** (5216 Montrose; 713–284–8250; www.camh.org) just across Montrose Boulevard. You can't miss the gleaming corrugated steel that forms the skin of the wedge-shaped CAM building. Inside, who knows what you'll find? Exhibitions here are guaranteed to tease and seduce all your senses, like the recent installation that featured a sensual stroll through glowing nylon "membranes." The CAM also boasts one of the most interesting museum shops in town, a great place to pick up offbeat souvenirs or gifts: a teapot with hands and feet or clocks with eyes. Don't miss it.

DAY TWO: afternoon

LUNCH

Just as visual overload threatens to swamp your senses, beat a sensible retreat to the Warwick for a long, soothing lunch at **The Terrace on Main,** the hotel's newest restaurant, located just off the gorgeous lobby. Take a load off and settle in for some serious pampering in this elegant little room or dine outside on the namesake terrace. The restaurant offers what may be the best BLT in town, certainly the most elegant, sandwiched between crisp cheddar-cheese waffles and drenched with a drinkably good basil mayonnaise. Or share a plate of tender smoked salmon on toasted brioche, garnished with silky peach halves lavished with vodka cream and black caviar.

After lunch you'll spend the afternoon exploring the cool interiors of the Houston **Museum of Natural Science** (One Hermann Circle Drive; 713–639– 4600) at the entrance to Hermann Park, just a block south of the Warwick. This lively, sprawling "edutainment" complex offers the **Burke Baker Planetarium,** the IMAX theater (713–639–IMAX) with its towering six-story screen, and the fabulous **Cockrell Butterfly Center,** in addition to its permanent exhibitions of dinosaurs, minerals, and oil and gas exploration technology.

Stop a moment at the museum doors to admire the giant-sized, fully functional sundial; then enter to buy your admission tickets. Your best strategy here is to pick the IMAX feature you'd like to see and secure tickets to it and then use your remaining time before and after the (usually) forty-five-minute film to explore the other attractions.

We're particularly fond of the glassed-in rain forest at the Cockrell Butterfly Center, fragrant with tropical blossoms and alive with "living jewels." Some 1,500 varieties of those brightly colored insects flutter overhead and sometimes settle entrancingly on your sleeves.

The butterflies are quite popular, and the center is often crowded on weekends, so to find peace and privacy you'll next take the elevator up to the new **McGovern Hall of the Americas.** This quiet, darkened gallery offers a dramatically lit collection of artifacts from the Americas, including the Maya, Inca, and Aztec cultures. You'll shiver at these sights from lost worlds and find several quiet alcoves for heartfelt embraces.

On your walk back to your hotel, say hello to the huge horse-back statue of General Sam Houston, our town's namesake. Ol' Sam's great bronze arm points toward the site of the Battle of San Jacinto some 20 miles away, a pivotal battle in the war for Texas independence.

DAY TWO: evening

DINNER

This evening you'll picnic splendidly on the grass at Hermann Park's **Miller Outdoor Theater** (Hermann Park, 100 Concert Drive; 713–284–8350; free) before delighting in the moonlit performance of your choice.

First stop by **Butera's Fine Foods & Deli** (4621 Montrose; 713–528–3737; inexpensive) to stock your picnic supplies. May we suggest a loaf of French bread, a crock of peppery pâté, and an iced bottle of champagne? Or perhaps some tender smoked salmon with capers and marinated onions or an assortment of fresh fruits with sweet whipped cream to dip them in? You're certain to find something irresistibly delicious in Butera's fragrant cases and shelves.

Do leave your car behind in the Warwick's parking garage and walk to the park. The stroll is short, well-lit, and safe, whereas the parking hassles around the theater are legendary.

Admission is free at Miller Outdoor Theater, but those auditorium-style seats under the soaring steel canopy require tickets. These may be picked up on performance day at the Miller box office (713–284–8352) between 11:30 A.M. and 1:00 P.M. or one hour before the show. Any remaining seats are released five minutes before the curtain, in case you didn't plan ahead.

Perches on the wide, grassy slope above are open to all on a first-come, first-served basis, but Houstonians have worked out a sort of understood seating protocol. If you brought lawn chairs along, you really should sit on the *left side* (facing the stage) of the hill. If you brought a blanket, then sit on the *right side*. One last word of advice: If you hope to follow every note or word of the performance, pick a spot lower down on the hill, closer to the stage. The crowd gets noisier the farther you move from the stage.

Now pick your place and spread out your blanket. Did you remember to pack mosquito repellent? Good, then there'll be no annoying whine to distract you from more important matters. As sunset gives way to moonrise and the music swells to a crescendo, you'll have all the accoutrements of romance you could wish.

DAY THREE: morning

BRUNCH

On slow, luxurious Sunday mornings, there's no better place in town to be than at the Warwick's justly famous Sunday brunch. The Warwick's ballroom is not a place for shorts and sandals, so slip into something just a little dressy. The tempting, buffet-style palette of dishes changes every week but is always accompanied by plenty of bubbly, if you're feeling festive.

You can change back into your civvies right after brunch for a leisurely Sunday in the park. The 400-plus green acres of Hermann Park spread out before you, with jogging trails, the **Hermann Park Golf Course** (6301 Golf Course Drive; 713–526–0077), and even horseback riding from the **Hermann Park Stables** (5716 Almeda; 713–529–2081).

You could even recapture a bit of your childhood at the **Houston Zoological Gardens** (1513 North MacGregor Drive; 713–284–8300), where more than 5,000 animals vie for your attention. Call ahead to find out the feeding schedule for the most appealing creatures, like the ponderous sea lions or frisky otters. Check out the rain-forest primate pavilion, the **Wortham World of Primates,** and the small-but-delightful **Kipp Aquarium.** Then rent a paddleboat built for two and cruise the pond, splashing in and out of the refreshing spray of the fountains. Wasn't it Simon and Garfunkel who sang "It's all happening at the zoo"? You will believe it's true, on a sunny Sunday afternoon. Make today a day of simple pleasures that you two will remember fondly, long after you've drawn this romantic weekend to a close.

Campus Capers and Village Life in the University

JUST WEST OF THE MUSEUM DISTRICT and south of Montrose, the area around Rice University and the quaint Village shopping area is one of Houston's loveliest neighborhoods. Beautiful homes—on a more human scale than the equally pricey River Oaks—are sited in the deep shade of ancient live oak trees, draped in Spanish moss. The *New York Times* dubbed North and South Boulevards here the "most beautiful residential streets in America."

PRACTICAL NOTES: Although the Rice University campus is open year-round, it's liveliest during the academic school year, which starts at the end of August and runs through May. You can check the Rice University Web site at www.rice.edu for a complete calendar of campus events that are open to the public, including film festivals, football games, concerts, lectures, and art exhibitions.

Bring your bicycles for a weekend of slow-paced exploring; these environs are most accessible and best appreciated from the saddle. Out-of-towners can rent bikes nearby at **Planetary Cycles** (4004 South Braeswood Boulevard; 713–668–2300); mountain or road bikes are available for $25 per day.

Rom**a**n**c**e

AT A GLANCE

♦ *Play hooky on Friday afternoon. Roam the* **Rice University** *campus (6100 Main Street; 713–348–0000; www.rice.edu), soaking up the architecture, art, and cheap draft beer. Make yourselves at home at the thoroughly modern* **Marriott Medical Center Hotel** *(6580 Fannin Street; 713–796–0080); then sup at oh-so-hip* **benjy's** *(2424 Dunstan; 713–522–7602) in the Village.*

♦ *Cycle the gracious, tree-lined avenues of* **West University Place** *with a strategic shopping stop at* **Surroundings** *(1710 Sunset Boulevard; 713–527–9838). Break for lunch at the* **Raven Grill** *(1916 Bissonnet Street; 713–521–2027) and then spend the afternoon browsing bookshelves at some of Houston's best independent bookstores.*

♦ *Dinner is fresh and casual at* **Goode Company Seafood** *(2621 Westpark Drive; 713–523–7154), followed by evening entertainment of your choice: music at the Shepherd School of Music, a film at the Rice Media Center, or intimate acting at Main Street Theater.*

♦ *Sunday is the only day to get seafood paella at* **Sabroso Grill** *(5510 Morningside Drive; 713–942–9900). Dig in early; then laze the afternoon away on the pleasant patio of* **The Ginger Man** *pub (5607½ Morningside Drive; 713–526–2770), in the company of seventy boutique beers on draft.*

DAY ONE: afternoon

Can you sneak out of work early this Friday? Then hurray! Play hooky and kick off your romantic escapades early, on Friday afternoon, when the **Rice University** campus (6100 Main Street; 713–348–0000; www.rice.edu) is at its "TGIF" peak. The campus is directly across Main Street from Hermann Park and the Texas Medical Center, where you'll be headquartered this weekend.

Take your camera along for a guided tour of the gorgeous Rice campus, all warm brick and sunny Mediterranean styling. Leave your car at the hotel or in designated visitor parking on campus. The best way to see these 285 leafy green acres is either by cycling or strolling, as there are no "public" roads through campus and parking is horribly congested. Contact the University Office of Admission (713–527–4036) to schedule your guided walking tour; during the school year, tours are routinely offered at 11:00 A.M. and 3:00 P.M.

Tour highlights will include **Rice Stadium,** which actually seats more fans than the nearby Astrodome, and the imposing **Lovett Hall,** where generations of gowned Houston brides have posed for keepsake photographs under its Southern Gothic archways. Behind Lovett is the formal **Engineering Quad;** look for its trademark campanile and the sculpture composed of three massive slabs of "Texas Pink" granite, the same stone used to build the State Capitol and the Galveston Seawall. Note the location of the **Alice Pratt Brown Hall,** home to the **Shepherd School of Music** and both Stude and Duncan concert halls, where you may return later this weekend for a concert or recital. The diminutive **Rice University Art Gallery** (6100 Main Street, Sewell Hall; 713–527–6069) is well worth a peek: It houses eclectic, even eccentric, exhibitions of cutting-edge contemporary art and student compositions. While you're on campus, pick up a copy of the school newspaper, the *Rice Thresher,* for a complete listing of the concerts, symposia, and lectures scheduled during your weekend.

If all this walking works up your thirst, by all means wind up your tour at one of Houston's least-known pubs: the well-hidden basement den called **Valhalla** (6100 Main Street, MS–530; 713–527–8101). The bargain-priced draft beer drops from 60 cents a cup to an incredibly cheap 40 cents on Friday afternoons. If you find the dim, dank rathskeller ambience under the chemistry hall rather too bohemian for your taste, sit outside under the trees. You two can toss a Frisbee and wax nostalgic about your own collegiate days.

DAY ONE: evening

Toward sunset wend your way to this weekend's home away from home at the **Houston Marriott Medical Center Hotel** (6580 Fannin Street; 713–796–0080; $79 to $159). This twenty-six-story tower in the heart of Houston's Medical Center is adjacent to all the university locales on this itinerary and features all the modern conveniences your comfort-craving hearts could desire: three surprisingly good restaurants, an indoor pool and health club, and multichannel cable/satellite TV, of course.

We particularly like the great views from the upper-floor suites, some of which feature in-room wet bars or even full kitchens. Weekend rates are especially attractive, a real bargain at $79 per night for comfortable standard rooms. An unexpected bonus: The management here is pet-permissive, in case you two can't bear to leave your beloved pooch at home.

Other conveniently located home bases for this itinerary include the **Warwick Hotel** (5701 Main Street; 713–526–1991; $179 to $254) and the **Patrician Bed and Breakfast** (1200 Southmore Boulevard; 800–553–5797 or 713–523–1114; $125).

DINNER

Tonight you'll join a select group of good-looking yuppie couples for a very hip, very good dinner at **benjy's** restaurant in the Village (2424 Dunstan; 713–522–7602; moderate). The setting is dramatically lit and industrially pared down, more like a chic art gallery than a dining room. Strike a pose upstairs in the loft-y lounge with a sleek, dry martini; then join in the downstairs dining fun with chef Aaron Guest's "New American" menu. Pay particular attention to those dishes from the wood-fired oven and the in-house smoked delicacies; otherwise, trust the chef's knack for inventive nightly specials.

Still wide awake? Then drop by **Dolce & Freddo** (5515 Kirby Drive at Sunset; 713–521•3260; inexpensive), just a few blocks away, for a sophisticated, sweet nightcap to sip and an intriguing crowd of night owls to keep you company. Choose from dozens of lickable flavors of gelattos or sorbettos or browse the wide selection of espressos, cordials, and cognacs. That should send you home with a warm glow . . .

DAY TWO: morning

BREAKFAST

This morning you'll bounce out of bed bright and early, ready for an energetic morning of bicycling. No? Then pull the covers over your heads at first light, instead, and engage in a lighthearted game of tickle and slap. Don't worry; you can make up lost time with a quickie continental breakfast in your room or at your hotel's **Deerfield Restaurant.**

Whenever you feel ready to face the world, slip into something out-doorsy, grab a street map, and mount your bicycles for a riding tour of the gracious tree-lined avenues of **West University Place.** You can shortcut across the Rice campus or skirt its perimeter by cycling northeast along Main Street, then turning left at Sunset Boulevard. From Sunset turn right (north) onto Mandell Street, cross Bissonnet Street, and then watch for the intersection with South Boulevard.

Romance shopper's alert: If you (accidentally?) pass your turnoff at Mandell Street and stay on Sunset riding west for only 2 more blocks, you'll find **Surroundings** (1710 Sunset Boulevard; 713–527–9838). Robert and Susan Hawkins, a husband-and-wife team, have lovingly assembled an exotic pan-global collection of art and artifacts, home decor items, and furnishings with which to feather your nest. You'll love the whimsical furniture hand-painted by Houstonian David Marsh, but the Chinese lacquer boxes or San Blas Indian–embroidered molas are more likely to fit in your bicycle's basket.

Turn right (east) on **South Boulevard**—and try not to tumble over the handlebars in amazement when you encounter the green-lawned splendor of this neighborhood. A wide, grassy esplanade divides the little-used traffic lanes, shaded by the gnarled limbs of live oak trees draped with Spanish moss. The most impressive homes are between West Boulevard and Parkway Drive; when you reach Parkway, turn left (north) to find South's sister street, **North Boulevard.** Turn left again to follow North Boulevard back toward your starting point.

The remaining neighborhood streets are beautiful, too, if less jaw-dropping than North and South Boulevards; ride and explore at your leisure. We recommend a lazy, looping route that ultimately returns you to Bissonnet Street between Woodhead and Hazard Streets around lunchtime.

DAY TWO: afternoon

LUNCH

By now you two will be more than ready—may we say, ravenous?—for lunch at the **Raven Grill** (1916 Bissonnet Street; 713–521–2027;

moderate). This cozy neighborhood eatery is aptly named after the nearby Edgar Allan Poe Elementary School and is restfully decorated in shades of sage green and cream, punctuated here and there with images of its totem feathered friend. You'll love nibbling on sinful treats like the crisply fried poblano pepper and onion rings or the hearty mesquite-grilled burgers. And when it comes to desserts, heck, you've earned it! Get two spoons and dive into the high-intensity Chocolate Nevermore, a triple-threat chocolate cake layered with chocolate mousse and topped with chocolate ganache.

After lazing over your coffee cups, set out for the shopping paradise known as the Village. On cycles you'll feel so much smarter than your fellow car-bound shoppers, jockeying grimly for those few parking spaces. While you could look for anything imaginable in this arcaded wonderland of more than 300 boutiques—gourmet foods and coffees, exotic beads and jewelry, or wonderfully scented bath goodies, to name just a few—we recommend you devote your afternoon to books.

The Village neighborhood houses some of Houston's best independent bookstores, several of them along the same Bissonnet Street you're on right now, the others across from the Village Arcade on University Boulevard. Avid collectors of signed, rare, and/or first edition books will get sweaty palms in the hushed, mahogany-shelved rooms of the **Detering Book Gallery** (2311 Bissonnet Street; 713–526–6974), where the very best stuff is secreted away upstairs, just waiting for you to covet it. Or perhaps you crave edgy, contemporary poetry to read aloud to your beloved? Then the well-lit intellectual's mecca at **Brazos Bookstore** (2421 Bissonnet Street; 713–523–0701) will make both your hearts beat faster. If you're mystery buffs, you'll thrill to the packed shelves of **Murder By The Book** (2342 Bissonnet Street; 713–524–8597).

Lovers of all things Britannic will find the shelves of their dreams at the **Book Collector** (2347 University Boulevard; 713–661–2665), as well as a fascinating collection of tiny toy soldiers. Don't laugh: Full-grown adults gather here every month or two to stage miniature battles on the brick patio. Your last stop should be the rambling **Half Price Books** (2537 University Boulevard; 713–524–6635), because even if you resist all temptation up to this point, you will both certainly cave in to Half Price's incredible jumble of marked-down new and used books, CDs, and calendars. No one has any idea what's on all these shelves, so don't even ask. The thrill here is in the hunt.

DAY TWO: evening

On your return to the Marriott, cool down with a leisurely dip in the hotel's swimming pool and then head to your room or suite for a steamy, soapy shower together. (If you forgot to pack your loofah and scented soaps, stop by the lobby-level gift shop on the way up.)

DINNER

Don't worry about dressing up tonight. The code is as casual as the seafood is fresh at **Goode Company Seafood** (2621 Westpark Drive at Kirby; 713–523–7154; moderate), a restaurant cleverly housed in a silver-sided railroad car. Ask for one of the cushy upholstered booths by the window, the better to see your loved one's smiling face over that steaming bowl of gumbo. Jim Goode's menu covers the Gulf Coast from Louisiana through Texas to Mexico. We're awfully fond of his mesquite-grilled catches, whether it be catfish or jumbo shrimp, but do check the blackboard for the daily special. Polish off a monstrous piece of his signature pecan pie if you can; better make that two forks, kids.

If you've aimed for an early dinner, there'll be plenty of time for some highbrow entertainment tonight, at very low cost. Make your plans depending on what's playing on the Rice University campus and what tickles your fancy, as a couple. We like the intimate operatic or chamber music experience at the **Shepherd School of Music**. The auditorium of the **Rice Media Center** (2100 University Boulevard at Stockton, entrance #8; 713–527–4882) is less posh but offers a compelling roster of independent and foreign "art" films. Events at either venue are often free, or at least *very* inexpensive compared with the big-league stages around town. You might also check the schedule for the **Main Street Theater** (2540 Times Boulevard; 713–524–6706; $5 to $20); their

Village-area theater seats just under one hundred patrons, whereas the nearby Chelsea Market facility holds a cozy 180 customers or so.

DAY THREE: morning

BREAKFAST

 Only on Sundays can you get Arturo Boada's seductive seafood paella at **Sabroso Grill** (5510 Morningside Drive; 713–942–9900; inexpensive), so this morning you'll sleep in, check out, and then head back to the Village for an eye-opening plateful. Saffron rice cooked al dente is generously heaped with a garlicky tangle of tender calamari, briny mussels, jumbo shrimp, and firm chunks of redfish, topped with fistfuls of chopped red-ripe Roma tomatoes and green onions. Definitely don't be late—the paella hits the plates starting at 11:00 A.M. and often sells out in a couple of hours. Would a juicy passion-fruit margarita be too scandalous at this hour? You decide.

Another coin toss will be in order for this afternoon's agenda. Shall you sit on the pleasant patio of **The Ginger Man** pub (5607½ Morningside Drive; 713–526–2770), just across the street from Sabroso? If darts are your game of choice, you might prefer to stay indoors and toss a few companionable rounds of cricket. Either way, there's something about seventy brands of boutique beer on tap and a shady picnic table that's just guaranteed to induce a mellow sense of well being, both with each other and the world.

Glamour and Glitz at the Galleria

OUSTON'S GALLERIA IS LIKE AN EMERALD CITY within our city, a glittering capital of world famous, world-class shopping and elegant restaurants, populated by a well-heeled clientele from all over the globe. With sixteen million guests flocking through each year, you'll hear more different languages spoken here than at the United Nations, and the lingua franca is the color of your money, darlings.

Pish posh, you say, how could shopping be romantic? Try Tiffany's, we say, or Fred Joaillier or Godiva Chocolatiers. Too sexy for your clothes? Not at Versace, Armani, Gucci, or Dolce & Gabbana, to say nothing of Saks Fifth Avenue, Neiman Marcus, and Lord & Taylor. Combine the heady atmosphere of luxury goods with fine food, prime wines, and pampering service, and you've got a sybaritic weekend getaway you won't soon forget.

PRACTICAL NOTES: Of course the most magical time to visit the Galleria district is during the Christmas holiday season. The merchants' association pulls out all the stops for a monthlong Christmas extravaganza, complete with choir concerts, parades, and tree-lighting ceremonies both indoors and out that attract thousands of visitors. Prevent heartbreak: Book your holiday trip early.

DAY ONE: afternoon

Surprise your sweetie with a limousine pickup to start your luxury weekend on just the right note of opulence. Make the arrangements

Romance AT A GLANCE

◆ Hire a limousine for an extravagant ride to your unforgettable weekend; hang out elegantly, as our former President George Bush did, at **The Houstonian Hotel, Club & Spa** (111 North Post Oak Lane; 713–680–2626 or 800–231–2759).

◆ Shop till you drop at the world-famous **Galleria Shopping Center** (5015 Westheimer Road; 713–622–0663). Pose for souvenir photos at the Williams Tower Park **Water Wall.**

◆ Rock on at the **Billy Blues BBQ Bar & Grill** (6025 Richmond; 713–266–9294) for hot Texas BBQ, cold beers, and a spacious dance floor.

◆ Wind up your weekend with luxurious spa pampering—massages and manicures—or ruin those nails climbing the rock walls at **The Houstonian.**

through a local service like **Uptown Galleria Towncar** (3303 South Rice Avenue; 713–784–1655). Plot a scenic route from your loved one's abode, or from either of Houston's airports, to The Houstonian; ask the limousine service to include fresh flowers and chilled champagne for a special touch. Then roll up the privacy glass separating the two of you from your discreet driver and do whatever seems wildly decadent . . . within the limits of good taste, of course!

DAY ONE: evening

Your most difficult task this weekend will be forcing yourself to leave the luxurious grounds of **The Houstonian Hotel, Club & Spa** (111 North Post Oak Lane; 713–680–2626 or 800–231–2759; www.houstonian.com; $139 to $425). This four-star resort was the residence of former President George Bush, who should certainly know how to pick a hotel. It's only a stone's throw from one of Houston's busiest freeways, Loop 610, but the forested eighteen-acre grounds insulate you completely from such weary realities as commuting. Here you can frolic in any of three outdoor, heated pools; play golf, tennis, basketball, or squash; practice your tai chi; climb rocks; or wander well-groomed nature trails.

We love The Houstonian's "hideaway" weekend plans, each of which includes breakfast for two and the use of the health and fitness facility, one of the finest in Texas. The tariff—including all

taxes—is $175 per night in a deluxe room; add champagne, choco-
late-dipped strawberries, and truffles for $215 per night; include
those same delicacies and upgrade to an executive suite for $359 per
night.

DINNER

In terms of sheer "wow" factor, it's hard to trump the breathtaking
drama of **Americas** (1800 Post Oak Boulevard; 713–961–1492;
expensive; reservations recommended) in the Pavilion; even better,
The Houstonian's shuttle will chauffeur you there and back. In a
sensuous palette of exotic wood and textured slate, voluptuous
blown-glass lamps descend from soaring ceilings amid a forest of
mosaic-tiled trees. Only food as bold and brightly colored as
Michael Cordua's tropical pan-Latino cuisine could hope to compete with such a setting; as in Gambas Encaramanoladas (colossal
shrimp encrusted with yuca, black beans, and chorizo) or Cerdo
Relleno (roasted pork tenderloin rolled and filled with fresh corn
and cheese pudding), or the extraordinary Churrasco steak that first
put him on the culinary map—succulent, char-grilled beef tenderloin, butterflied and bathed in garlicky chimichurri sauce. Americas
opened to immediate acclaim and national "best new restaurant"
status back in 1993; tonight you and your beloved will discover
what is still one of the most exciting dining experiences in the city.

DAY TWO: morning

BREAKFAST

Take advantage of your weekend hideaway package breakfast, served
either in your room or the pretty **Olivette** dining room. Either way,
you're both sure to be delighted by executive chef Jim Mills's
Mediterranean-influenced menu. You can be commendably health-
conscious or downright naughty; it's up to you.

After breakfast The Houstonian's private shuttle will whisk you
away to the **Galleria Shopping Center** (5015 Westheimer Road;
713–622–0663), just 2 miles south. Like the legendary Rodeo

Drive in Beverly Hills or Miami's Miracle Mile, Houston's Uptown/Galleria district, at the roaring junction of Westheimer and Loop 610, has to be experienced to be believed. Look overhead: Mirror-finished steel arches and space-age, tubular rings hover over the intersections. Even the traffic-signal lights and street signs are Jetson-mod ovals of black and silver. And you'd better wear your most comfortable shoes: The Galleria proper includes some 300 stores—plus an ice-skating rink and dozens of restaurants—in three mammoth, three-story complexes labeled Galleria I, II, and III. Once inside the doors, rely on well-designed maps and frequent information booths to keep from getting hopelessly lost; you two might want to agree upon a meeting place should you get separated.

DAY TWO: afternoon

LUNCH

At lunchtime the mind boggles at the number of restaurants. Without ever leaving the Galleria's premises, you can dine quickly and well. Your decision may rest on where you're shopping when hunger strikes. Sure, the **Cheesecake Factory** (ground level, next to Lord & Taylor; 713–840–0600) serves dozens of kinds of cheesecake but also decent burgers, sandwiches, salads, and pizzas. Down by the ice-skating rink, **La Madeleine French Bakery** (lower level; 713–993–0287) dishes up fresh, crusty breads, roasted chicken, and a nicely dressed Caesar salad. In the most soothing Galleria venue by far, the **Zen Café** (Lower level; 713–572–2376) treats you to sushi, teriyaki chicken, prettily steamed vegetables, and the *very* welcome suggestion that you remove your shoes.

Seasoned shoppers may scoff at the notion of stopping while there's still daylight left, but if you do escape the clamor of cash registers, a quiet stroll in the beautiful little park just behind the Galleria will refresh your senses. This three-acre gem of urban greenery is now officially known as the **Williams Tower Park** (2800 South Post Oak Boulevard), but try getting a Houstonian to call it that. To the natives one and all, it will always be known as it was christened: the Transco Tower Park.

Whatever you call the place, it's one of this city's premier photo opportunities. Since 1985, thousands of lovers have posed in front of the dramatic, drum-shaped Water Wall, where 11,000 gallons of water pour down the 64-foot vertical face every minute. Now it's your turn. You did bring your Instamatic, didn't you? Ask nicely, and a passerby will be glad to snap a shot of you together. Then summon your magic carpet, er, shuttle car, to ferry you back to The Houstonian.

DAY TWO: evening

DINNER

This evening we'll separate the real troopers from the couch potatoes. Are your hamstrings crying "Uncle"? Are your shoulders threatening to separate from the weight of all those shopping bags? In that case you two should schedule massages in the health club or, at the very least, a long, long soak in that heated pool or whirlpool. Relax—your reward is a late, secluded supper at **Olivette,** right in the privacy of your hotel. Don't fret—it is one of the best venues around, and despite its marvelous cuisine and notable wine list, rarely crowded in the evenings. For sheer pampering it's hard to beat the pan-roasted lobster basted with whiskey-scented butter or, if you prefer, go with something simple and soothing, like the lemon-grilled chicken or a heavenly big bowl of soup.

But if you two are tireless, energized by love and sexy new clothes, tonight might be just the night to go out and *party*. Just a short taxi ride from The Houstonian, west of the Galleria, you'll find a dining and dancing venue that really rocks: the **Billy Blues BBQ Bar & Grill** (6025 Richmond; 713-266-9294; moderate), marked by a you-can't-miss-it giant sculpted saxophone. Every night of the week you'll find gutsy Texas BBQ and ice-cold, long-neck beers; the music roams the dial from blues, of course, to swing to R&B to jazz. Call ahead to find out who's playing, if you care; we like Austin's Marcia Ball best but are also fond of hometown hero Ezra Charles. You can dance as long as you like, or until 2:00 A.M. on weekend nights, whichever comes first.

DAY THREE: morning

Whatever the outcome of last night's momentous decision—dining, or dining and dancing?—today is another sunny day. After breakfasting in your room, we suggest you make the best use of The Houstonian's spa facilities today.

For him or for her, there are dozens of delightful ways to be pampered and indulged: massages, manicures, pedicures, facials, baths, body treatments, aromatherapy, and makeovers, to name just a few.

Does that sound too tame for you two? Then consider a morning's workout rock climbing, for real full-body engagement. The Houstonian's indoor wall offers four challenging levels (and a soft foam mat to cushion your falls) for a nominal sum of $5.00 per hour. Certification courses are available; talk to the instructor for details.

As you are kneaded on the massage table, or stretching for that next rock grip, you two may reflect that perhaps it's true that money can't buy you love. Share a knowing grin with your partner, because what you two *have* learned this weekend is that luxury makes lovely company for your love affair already in full bloom.

Sports and Celluloid at Greenway Plaza

B Y DAY THE GREENWAY PLAZA AREA of Houston is a hive of worker bees, a bustling cluster of ten major commercial towers on the Southwest Freeway (US–59) at Buffalo Speedway. So what's the draw for you two? By night the **Compaq Center Arena** buzzes with 17,000 sports fans, cheering on our home teams like the two-time NBA champion Houston Rockets, the three-time WNBA champion Comets, the Aeros (IHL), and the Thunderbears (AFL). Other Compaq Center events range from rock concerts to figure skating to three-ring circuses.

And it's not all about spectator sports, either. Nearby you two will find a wealth of "interactive" evening entertainments, with cinema, nightclub, and dancing choices all within walking distance of the plaza and with the art galleries and famed restaurants of the "Upper Kirby" district near at hand. So who said Greenway Plaza is strictly business? Nobody who's been there, that's for sure.

PRACTICAL NOTES: Time your trip around the sporting event of your choice. To find out who's playing, contact the Compaq Center Arena (10 East Greenway Plaza; 713–843–3995; www.compaq center.com). All tickets may be purchased at the Compaq Center box office (713–843–3995) or through Ticketmaster (713–629–3700). We've customized this itinerary for a Friday-night game, but you can easily tailor it to fit your desires.

*R*omance
AT A GLANCE

◆ Kick off your shoes and your workaday blues for a beer-and-mudbug feast at the **Ragin' Cajun Restaurant** (4302 Richmond Avenue; 713–623–6321).

◆ Check into high-rise executive splendor at the **Renaissance Houston Hotel** (6 East Greenway Plaza; 713–629–1200). Then, unlike the 16,998 car-bound fans, you two will simply walk to the sporting event of your choice at the **Compaq Center.** If you find you need a little nibble after the game, stop by **Carrabba's** (3115 Kirby Drive; 713–522–3131) for an upscale snack and some celebrity spotting.

◆ After breakfast at your hotel, conduct an "art crawl" along the galleries of Colquitt Street. Lunch on gourmet fast food at **Cafe Express** (3200 Kirby Drive; 713–522–3994); then sneak around back to the **Dessert Gallery Bakery & Café** (3200 Kirby; 713–522–9999) for a decadent sweet—or two.

◆ Take in a flick at the (really) underground cinema, the **Landmark Greenway 3** (5 East Greenway Plaza; 713–626–0402). Or if mainstream's more your game, the spanking-new **Edwards Greenway Grand Palace 24** (3839 Weslayan; 713–871–8880) is just around the corner.

◆ Pull out all the stops at **Los Andes** (3700 Richmond; 713-622-2686), a South American restaurant that magically transforms itself into a glamorous Havana-style nightclub, where you can salsa the sultry night away.

◆ Sleep in, take a swim, and then head over to **Goode Company Hamburgers & Taqueria** (4902 Kirby Drive; 713–520–9153) for a soul-satisfying Tex-Mex breakfast finale.

DAY ONE: evening

DINNER

Lose those workaday neckties and pantyhose and kick off your weekend early with happy hour at a real down-home dive, the **Ragin' Cajun Restaurant** (4302 Richmond Avenue; 713–623–6321; inexpensive). At the height of crawfish season, usually during May and June, you two will join celebrants from all over the city to feast in paper-bibbed splendor on bright-red, boiled mudbugs, washed down with plenty of ice-cold beer. If you don't know the proper procedure to eat a crawfish, one of your newfound friends will no doubt be pleased to demonstrate. Off-season, the New Orleans–style muffaletta sandwiches, red beans and rice, and seafood gumbo are all equally popular. Like the Crescent City itself, this is a rollicking rendezvous that'll help you check your cares at the door.

Afterward head against the stream of rush-hour traffic east along Richmond to the **Renaissance Houston Hotel** (6 East Greenway Plaza; 713–629–1200; standard rooms $79 to $159). Okay, so the twenty-story, black-glass tower looks like a businessman's hotel, and—unless the sight of glossy leather briefcases and ubiquitous cell phones turns you on—you might well wonder, where's the romance? The beauty is that this modern, comfortable hotel is practically deserted on the weekends, so you'll have the facilities, like the health club, sauna, and landscaped outdoor swimming pool, all to yourselves and at a bargain rate to boot. Standard rooms start as low as $79 for a weekend night.

If you two prefer to splurge, consider the seventeenth-floor Presidential Suite at $750 per night, instead. It's a palatial two-story suite with a spiral staircase leading from the downstairs parlor up to the bedroom, a whirlpool for two in the bath, and a dramatic view of the city lights below.

Then, sports fans, it's off to **Compaq Center** for the game. And here's a tip: When the on-court action slows, you can sneak away through the lowest-level bar into the echoing, empty halls beneath the stands. Talk about an exciting place for a passionate kiss, with the roar of a standing ovation above you? Gives us goosebumps just to think of it.

Should you find after the game that you require a bit more sustenance before retiring, **Carrabba's** (3115 Kirby Drive; 713–522–3131) is the late-night, postgame place to go. Fans stream in to conduct spirited postmortems, and the players as often show up, too. It's lively and boisterous and full of good-looking, happy people like you. Oh, and the food is very good, as well; tonight you might be most tempted by the highly snackable antipasti like fried calamari and wood-oven pizzas. It's too clamorous for quiet conversations, so substitute flirty glances or soulful gazes for those whispery sweet nothings.

DAY TWO: morning

Grab a quick breakfast bite at **Amelia's** in your hotel, a pleasant ground-story room overlooking the plaza's fountains and the pyramid-shaped skylights into the Greenway Concourse below. Today you two will spend your morning pleasantly gallery hopping along nearby Colquitt Street. To get there follow Richmond east to Kirby and turn left; then turn left again on Colquitt.

Over the years several galleries have gravitated to this short stretch of formerly residential street, making it terribly convenient for one-stop art shopping or just fascinating browsing. Start at the **Goldesberry Gallery** (2625 Colquitt; 713–528–0405), closest to Kirby, for an intriguing collection of one-of-a-kind art jewelry, and if you see an adornment you simply must have, do drop enough unsubtle hints to get it. **Barbara Davis Galleries** (2627 Colquitt; 713–520–9200) houses contemporary art, and the **Hooks-Epstein Gallery** (2631 Colquitt; 713–522–0718) specializes in representational art, sculpted or on paper. The **John Cleary Gallery** (2635 Colquitt; 713–524–5070) is devoted entirely to fine-art photography, both modern and vintage, whereas the **New Gallery** (2639 Colquitt; 713–520–7053) tends to large, abstract works, very contemporary. Other notable stops to immerse yourselves in artistic vision include the **Dean Day Gallery** (2707 Colquitt; 713–520–1021) and the **Moody Gallery** (2815 Colquitt; 713 526 9911).

DAY TWO: afternoon

LUNCH

Barely a block's stroll north of you on Kirby you'll find your lunch destination, **Cafe Express** (3200 Kirby Drive; 713–522–3994). Yes, you'll order your meal at the counter, but don't mistake this for a cookie-cutter fast-food emporium; this popular "speedy gourmet" outlet is the brainchild of respected local chef Robert Del Grande of Café Annie fame. Everything on the menu is fresh and fabulous, from the great bowls of pasta to the upscale burgers to the prettily-tossed Caesar salads. Find yourselves a patio table amid the other beautiful people and put your feet up, for a well-earned respite.

And for an afternoon delight, slip around the back of this same building to the **Dessert Gallery Bakery & Café** (3200 Kirby; 713–522–9999). All the pastries here are scrumptious, but perhaps the most seductive is suggestively named The Big O, a double-layered stack of creamy mousse filling, one dark and one white chocolate, both plentifully studded with crumbled Oreo cookies. Oh, indeed.

Postprandially, we propose the cool environs of an underground movie theater—perhaps literally—for the most romantic flick you can find. If your tastes tend to the highbrow and artistic, then the **Landmark Greenway 3** (5 East Greenway Plaza; 713–626–0402) in the Greenway underground concourse is for you. Prefer something a little more first-run mainstream, perhaps with a full dose of Hollywood special effects? Then try the **Edwards Greenway Grand Palace 24** just around the corner (3839 Weslayan and the Southwest Freeway, next to Compaq Center; 713–871–8880). In either case take advantage of the flickering darkness for some sweet petting . . .

When Is a Cigar Not Just a Cigar?

When a woman is smoking it, of course. The cigar craze that started in the mid-90s created an unexpected trend that really turned men's heads, as women began firing up their own stogies. Actresses Tia Carrere and Demi Moore, supermodel Linda Evangelista, and pop singer Madonna all lit up, at one time or another, and many men found this deeply sexy. If, daring duo, you decide to try puffing in tandem this special evening, do avoid the silly mistakes that will mark you as a rookie. Don't bite the cigar end off (that's what cutters are for); don't knock the ash off until it measures at least an inch long (then gently tip it into an ashtray); and, for goodness sake, don't inhale! That green-around-the-gills look is a dead giveaway. For your maiden voyage we recommend Romeo y Julietas, *of course; later you can exchange the rings or press them into your scrapbook.*

DAY TWO: evening

DINNER

Back at the hotel put on your sexiest, slinkiest attire, darlings, and don't skimp on the glitz. Think of Madonna as Eva Peron paired with Antonio Banderas, for tonight you'll dine on sultry South American cuisine and dance to salsa music that's red-hot and live at **Los Andes** (3700 Richmond;

713–622–2686; moderate). As a matter of fact, you might want to first stop by the **Greenway Pipe & Tobacco** shop in the underground concourse (5 East Greenway Plaza; 713–626–1613), as cigars are welcomed in this Havana-style restaurant and nightclub.

As you nibble teasingly at ceviche, cazuela de mariscos, or tenderloin basted in chimichurri sauce, you'll feel the erotic tension building toward the moment the band swings into the irresistible Latin rhythms of salsa, merengue, and cumbia music. The sophisticated dance crowd arrives fashionably late; by the time dinner is cleared and the floor is full you'll find yourselves in the thick of it.

Afterward you'll welcome the cool night air as you stroll back to the hotel. Perhaps a nightcap in the clubby **Lobby Bar** could be fitted into your agenda, or maybe you'll take your drinks up to your room. Hang the DO NOT DISTURB sign on the door, turn out the lights . . . and admire the view.

DAY THREE: morning

BREAKFAST

You worked so hard dancing till the wee hours last night, a sleep-in is definitely in order this morning. Rise and shine with a quick restorative dip in the hotel swimming pool before checking out. Then head on over to **Goode Company Hamburgers & Taqueria** (4902 Kirby Drive; 713–520–9153), one of Houston's Sunday-morning institutions. No, you're not limited to hamburgers or tacos; the weekend breakfast menu includes longshoreman-sized platters of spicy huevos rancheros and migas, fresh tortillas, home-style sausage, and creamy grits. Other couples on the breezy patio and around the central fountain will be comparing notes on the weekend's successes; will any of them have smiles as smugly satisfied as yours?

Sweet and Slow in the Suburbs

The Good Life on the Greens in The Woodlands

HERE DO WELL-HEELED HOUSTONIANS GO when they want to get away from it all without leaving city amenities behind? Only 27 miles north of downtown Houston lies The Woodlands, an exclusive "master-planned" community with 27,000 acres of manicured lawns, fragrant pine trees, rippling lakes, and championship golf courses. At its heart is the four-star **Executive Conference Center and Resort,** the centerpiece of your sybaritic weekend.

Couples that play together will delight in the tournament golf courses, tennis courts, swimming pools, and leafy miles of hike-and-bike trails. Après-sport perks include a full-service spa, his-and-hers fitness centers, and three on-site gourmet restaurants. And if you can bear to leave your snug lakeside retreat for even a few hours, the resort's shuttle service will whisk you away to an evening of music at the neighborhood's gem of a performing arts center, the outdoor **Cynthia Woods Mitchell Pavilion.** From the Spice Girls to the Houston Symphony— the Pavilion is the Houston Symphony's summer home, by the way— you're sure to find just the right music for your romantic agenda.

PRACTICAL NOTES: The resort's Tournament Players Course is home to the PGA Tour's annual **Shell Houston Open.** If you're devoted members of the golfing gallery, this could be fairway heaven, provided you make your plans well in advance and don't mind paying a peak-season premium price to rub elbows with tour

Romance AT A GLANCE

◆ *Pamper yourselves at a four-star sport and spa resort, **The Woodlands Executive Conference Center and Resort** (2301 North Millbend Drive; 800–433–2624 or 281–367–1100). Dine in continental style at the resort's flagship restaurant, the **Glass Menagerie**.*

◆ *Choose a championship eighteen-hole golf course or meet on the tennis courts for a love match. Lunch afterward by the greens at the **Knickers Bar and Grill** or go Mediterranean at **Spartilo**, both part of the resort's impressive culinary lineup. Finish your day by getting rubbed, buffed, and burnished at the top-notch spa facility. Swedish massage, anyone?*

◆ *Slip away for a northern Italian dinner for two, preferably on the patio by torchlight, at nearby **Amerigo's Grille** (25250 Grogan's Park Drive; 281–362–0808). Then let the resort's shuttle service whisk you hassle-free to a musical performance at the **Cynthia Woods Mitchell Pavilion** (2005 Lake Robbins Drive; 281–363–3300).*

◆ *After a refreshing swim in the resort pool, ease into the excellent Sunday brunch hosted by the "on campus" **Glass Menagerie**.*

celebrities. On the other hand, if you two crave a quiet retreat far from the madding crowd, pick one of the resort's off-peak periods, usually during the months of January and February, or the long days of summer in June, July, and August. Insiders tell us bargain room rates abound while the world plays elsewhere.

And while laying your loving plans, be sure to call the **Cynthia Woods Mitchell Pavilion** at (281) 363–3300 to choose the musical performance of your choice.

DAY ONE: afternoon

To get to **The Woodlands Executive Conference Center and Resort** (2301 North Millbend Drive; 800–433–2624 or 281–367–1100; $278 to $338), your best bet is to leave downtown Houston by mid-afternoon ahead of the snarled traffic heading north at rush hour. Take Interstate 45 North to exit 73, Rayford-Sawdust Road. Turn left under the freeway and stay on Rayford-Sawdust (which becomes Grogan's Mill Road) through seven traffic lights to North Millbend. Then just follow the signs to the resort.

Special resort packages include unlimited championship golf and tennis deals, spa weekends, and a romantic getaway bundle that includes a buffet-style breakfast in **The Woodlands Dining Room** and dinner at the **Glass Menagerie** restaurant in the room price ($278 per couple, per night). All the resort's rooms are grouped in handsome stone "lodges," with views over the greens, the surrounding woods, or the waters of man-made Lake Harrison; many have private patios. If you want to splurge memorably, consider a bilevel honeymoon suite ($338 per night), with a spiral staircase leading enticingly to the bedroom upstairs and a small kitchenette downstairs, great for rustling up simple midnight snacks.

Once you've checked in, there's plenty of time before dinner to amble round the grounds of your weekend retreat. Stop by the pro shop to pick up a map of the resort and choose one of the many hike-and-bike trails to explore. (And while you're here, remember to pick your court or tee times for tomorrow.) In the surrounding woods you'll find plenty of pine-scented glades, almost all blessedly private, for some serious face-to-face time; between the breeze and the birdsong, you'll feel those urban tensions melting away.

Then head for **Woody's Lounge** in time to catch the sunset over the peaceful waters of Lake Harrison, and offer a genteel toast to your mutual good fortune.

DAY ONE: evening

DINNER

Slip into something elegantly comfortable and stroll to dinner tonight at the resort's **Glass Menagerie** restaurant. The continental menu changes with the seasons, but the beef and seafood entrees are always top-notch.

DAY TWO: morning

BREAKFAST

Rise and shine this morning for an early breakfast in **The Woodlands Dining Room,** the central dining facility of the resort.

You'll feel healthier immediately as you choose from the extensive buffet of fresh fruit, whole-grain cereals, and breads hot from the oven; or go the devil-may-care route with a cheese-stuffed omelet and a rasher of thick-sliced bacon.

Then gather your rackets or clubs, gird yourselves in your most fetching resort sportswear, and let the games begin. Of the two eighteen-hole golf courses open to resort guests, golfers will find the Tournament Course more challenging than the one recently rechristened as The Pines. If your games need improvement, schedule lessons or sign up for the skills clinics available for both golf and tennis players, with instruction provided by resident pros.

DAY TWO: afternoon

LUNCH

If you've spent the morning golfing, try the **Knickers Bar and Grill** at the Tournament Players Course for a moderately priced light-lunch selection of soups, salads, and sandwiches. We also like **Spartilo** for its casual Mediterranean pasta or deep-dish pizza, hot from the wood-burning oven.

After lunch spend a rejuvenating afternoon at the resort's spa. Picture yourselves wreathed in clouds of sauna steam or soothing away muscle kinks in the hydrojet whirlpools. Or treat yourselves to herbal baths followed by a Swedish massage. Even beauty services are on offer: manicures, pedicures, and facials are yours for the asking (and for a fee, of course). You'll both be burnished, glowing, and deeply relaxed by dinnertime, guaranteed.

DAY TWO: evening

DINNER

Unless you want to make a less-than-satisfying meal of popcorn and nachos at tonight's concert, we recommend an early dinner

Gracing the Greens:
Ladies Who Golf

Olympic medalist and pioneering women's golf champion "Babe" Didrikson Zaharias hailed from nearby Port Arthur, Texas. Feisty, flamboyant, and the first female athlete to be famous by a single name, Babe's sports prowess and hunger for victory was rivaled only by her appetite for unconventional romance, according to latter-day biographers. She may have been the biggest name in the fledgling LPGA back in 1949 but was by no means the first female to take to the links: In the sixteenth century Mary, Queen of Scots coined the term "caddies" for the young scions of French nobility who admiringly followed her around the course, while Edith Cummings, an amateur champion of the Roaring Twenties, was said to have inspired F. Scott Fitzgerald to create Daisy, Gatsby's unattainable true love in The Great Gatsby.

before the show. Of course, you can dine "on campus" at the resort or, for a change of pace, drive just a few minutes away to **Amerigo's Grille** (25250 Grogan's Park Drive; 281–362–0808; expensive). Here, you'll love the seating on the dramatically torchlit patio as much as the classy northern Italian menu—especially that signature wild-boar chop; even better, both the service and the wine cellar are first-class.

Rather than driving on to the show afterward, consider returning to the resort and requesting that the resort's shuttle service ferry you to the **Cynthia Woods Mitchell Pavilion** (2005 Lake Robbins Drive; 281–363–3300) instead. The ride is only $10 per couple each way and will save you enormous parking headaches.

The most comfortable, sheltered seating at the Pavilion is in the arena chairs under the soaring canopy, but we've always thought it more romantic to spread a blanket on the grassy hill above. Suit yourself and the weather, but don't try to smuggle in a bottle of bubbly or even a can of insect repellent: All that stuff's for sale inside. Now sit back and enjoy the music, the stars overhead, and each other's company.

DAY THREE: morning

BREAKFAST

Take it slow and easy this morning. Start with a dip in the resort swimming pool; then lounge in side-by-side chaises to soak up some sunshine. That will put you in the right mood for the luxurious Sunday brunch at the **Glass Menagerie**. After an active weekend like this, you can relax and indulge in the rich selection of frilly eggs, creamy sauces, and tempting pastries. Toast each other with your eyes—and maybe a bit of bubbly, too—to bring your spa retreat weekend to a satisfyingly genteel close.

FOR MORE ROMANCE

If you'd like to do a little exploring while you're out in this neck of the woods, so to speak, head over to **Old Town Spring,** which is practically next door. Use the suggestions from Itinerary 15 to spend the afternoon shopping and dining in the restored village's pleasantly old-fashioned atmosphere.

The Picturesque "Piney Woods" of Old Town Spring

NOT FAR FROM THE WOODLANDS is a completely different sort of getaway destination, a fanciful escape into Texas's small-town past. Old Town Spring is a restored turn-of-the-century railroad village with cobblestone streets, carriage tours, and arts and crafts shops. The historic community centers on a two-story former hotel and saloon now reincarnated as a restaurant. This weekend you'll relax country-style at one of the area's oldest bed-and-breakfast inns, a former family farm, and browse the nearby antiques stores, art galleries, and small museums.

To get to Old Town Spring from Houston, take the Hardy Toll Road north to the FM–1960 exit and stay on the feeder road into town; or take Interstate 45 North to exit 70A, turn east at the traffic light onto Spring-Cypress Road, and follow it 1 mile into town.

PRACTICAL NOTES: Holiday spirits abound at Christmastime, when the village is transformed into a shopper's paradise during the **Home for the Holidays** celebration. Almost 200 shops in the 10-block restored area sport festive decorations, and barbershop quartets and carolers sing from the street corners. The event kicks off in mid-November with a parade and tree-lighting ceremony and runs through the shopping days of December.

Also popular is Old Town Spring's **Crawfish Festival,** featuring music and "mudbugs" for two weekends in May, and **Old Town**

Romance AT A GLANCE

◆ Trade in your urban blues for a restorative weekend on a 150-year-old family farm at the **McLachlan Farm Bed & Breakfast** (24907 Hardy; 800–382–3988 or 281–350–2400).

◆ Share a quiet supper at **Teddi's Restaurant & Tea Room** (9001 Louetta Road; 281–251–5055) in Old Town Spring.

◆ Enjoy a farmhand's hearty breakfast at your inn; then explore the road less traveled along one of the farm's pine-needled walking trails.

◆ Head into town for lunch at **Nielsen's Bakery** (26830 I–45 North at Rayford-Sawdust; 281–363–3354), followed by an afternoon of shopping in the quaint streets of the village.

◆ Dine at the historic **Wunsche Brothers Cafe & Saloon** (103 Midway Street, 281–350–1902), where you'll find a pleasing medley of Czech country food and Country Western music, with maybe some humorous story swapping thrown in for good measure.

Spring Heritage Days, celebrated at the end of September, when antique automobiles and performers in vintage dress make the past seem closer than ever. If you two plan to visit Spring at these popular festival times, do make your reservations early.

DAY ONE: evening

To find the **McLachlan Farm Bed & Breakfast** (24907 Hardy; 800–382–3988 or 281–350–2400; $85 to $100), head straight through Old Town Spring toward the railroad tracks. Just before the crossing, turn right on Hardy Road. The farm is 1 mile south; look for the sign on the right; then turn down the quarter-mile-long graveled driveway.

At the end of this tranquil road is a welcoming sight: the rambling yellow farmhouse, shaded by sycamores and pecans, which has been in the family of your hospitable hosts, Jim and Joycelyn Clairmonte, for almost 150 years. We like the ground floor Mac Room ($85 per night) best for its floor-to-ceiling bay window and beautiful view of the woods just outside; the queen-size canopy bed is prettily trimmed with grapevines and flowers. Ask for the special occasion package ($30), and the Clairmontes will have chilled gourmet cider, freshly cut flowers, and bubble bath waiting for your arrival.

If there's daylight left after your check-in, do be sure to explore the garden and its Victorian rose arbor. Scene of many weddings, this arbor is the perfect backdrop for a keepsake photograph of the two of you.

DINNER

You'll drive into town tonight for a quiet supper at **Teddi's Restaurant & Tea Room** (9001 Louetta Road; 281–251–5055; moderate). Though you're far from the shore, many of our favorite meals here center on the continental-style seafood dishes, like the seafood linguine in a hearty red marinara sauce or the halibut fillet topped with shrimp in a decadently rich cream sauce.

Back at the farm relax arm in arm into the creaking wooden swing, dangling invitingly from the rafters of the wraparound porch, and listen to the crickets in the warm night. Later, you two might put that bubble bath to good use . . . by candlelight, of course.

DAY TWO: morning

BREAKFAST

Start your day with a hearty country-style breakfast at your inn; then spend the morning communing with nature and each other as you hike one of the farm's wooded trails. Well-marked and softly cushioned with pine needles, these secluded paths offer equal opportunities for bird-watching and making out. Take your binoculars along if you're interested in the former, or perhaps a stadium blanket for the latter.

DAY TWO: afternoon

LUNCH

It's a good thing you two are already wearing your walking shoes, the better to shop your way across Old Town Spring this afternoon. Start by heading back into town for lunch at **Nielsen's Bakery** (26830 I–45 North at Rayford-Sawdust; 281–363–3354; inexpensive). The ever-changing menu of soups, salads, and sandwiches will fortify you for the afternoon's adventures; don't miss their famous potato salad dressed with house-made mayo, and try the piled-high turkey sandwich.

The Romance of the Railroad

Platted by the Houston and Great Northern Railroad in 1873, Spring was a brawling railroad boomtown of hotels and honky-tonks by 1902. By the 1930s it busted flat, thanks to Prohibition, the Depression, and the transfer of the rail yard to Houston. But the tracks that first built the town of Spring, linking it to Houston, Galveston, and New Orleans, still run alongside the **Wunsche Brothers Cafe & Saloon.** *The occasional string of freight cars still rattles over those rails, provoking sweet nostalgia in listeners "of a certain age." No, it's not the double-pistoned "choo-choo" signature of the original iron horse, which has been displaced by diesel engines, but if you use your imaginations, you can almost hear it . . .*
Put a penny on the track anyway, just for luck.

The shops of Old Town Spring are bunched into an area no more than 10 blocks square, and many are housed in the historic homes, bank, and post office of the former railroad town. The concept has proved tremendously appealing to sentimental city folk. Where twenty years ago there were only ten stores, you'll now find almost 200. Town maps are readily available from merchants and the tiny **Spring Historical Museum** (403 Main Street; 281–651–0055).

We'll leave the exploring up to you two and your stamina, with just a few suggestions to get you started: **Maggie's** (111 Midway; 281–288–8816) offers upscale clothing, jewelry, and home decorations; **Goodwood's British Market** (216 Gentry; 281–288–7766) has, not surprisingly, a large selection of imported teas and teapots; whereas the **Amish Barn** (311-A Main Street; 281–651–9209) is a great place to find handmade Amish quilts, as well as jams and jellies. If a birdhouse fashioned to look like a New England church is your idea of yard elegance, you'll find it at **Metals, Petals & More** (26414 Preston; 281–528–8831), along with a whimsical collection of garden sculpture and raku pottery; and at the holidays don't miss **Gambrell's** (206 Main Street; 281–353–0800) "theme" trees and imported ornaments and nutcrackers. And history buffs will appreciate a stop at the **Civil War Museum** (206 Noble Street in Thyme Square; 281–288–7252), home to the 11th Texas Cavalry, a sponsor of historic reenactments during the Heritage festival.

DAY TWO: evening

DINNER

By the time evening comes, you'll be ready for two hearty down-home dinners at **Wunsche Brothers Cafe & Saloon** (103 Midway Street; 281–350–1902). Housed in the former hotel and saloon of Spring's railroad boomtown days, Wunsche Brothers dishes out history lessons along with its chicken-fried steaks and bratwurst. Flip over the menu to read the story of the building and its founding brothers, and admire the vintage photos lining the walls.

After dinner stick around for an evening's entertainment: local talent takes the stage weekend nights, telling tall tales and playing a toe-tapping selection of country-western and bluegrass favorites. You can hold hands under the table while sipping your cold, long-neck beers, and no one will mind a bit.

DAY THREE: morning

After a farewell breakfast at your inn, you might just kick back and enjoy one last morning of country peace and quiet, or you can drive just a bit farther north along Interstate 45 to **Tomball,** a town often described as a "collector's mecca" of antiques stores. Ask your innkeepers for town maps and sure-fire shopping suggestions.

Starlight Campgrounds:
BRAZOS BEND AND THE GEORGE RANCH

F OR CERTAIN SPECIAL COUPLES "wildlife" isn't found in a nightclub: The quintessential romantic getaway is a weekend spent embracing each other *and* nature, with nothing more than the branches of a live oak and a tent flap to separate you from the starry night sky.

Surprisingly few city campers have yet discovered the lush environs of **Brazos Bend State Park,** despite the fact that it's less than an hour's drive from Houston. Most weekends you'll have plenty of elbow room to ramble its secluded hike-and-bike trails or fish from the shady riverbanks.

And you're not condemned to truly roughing it when you can supplement your camp cooking with hearty meals at the nearby **George Ranch** or spend an evening stargazing through the high-tech research telescope of the **George Observatory.**

PRACTICAL NOTES: Call the state park system's camping center in Austin (512–389–8900) for campsite reservations. Primo times for Gulf Coast camping are the glorious days of early spring in March and April, when wildflowers and butterflies abound, or in fall, say late September and early October, when the nights begin to cool and the first flocks of migrating birds fill the clear skies. Spring and fall weather is famously changeable in Texas, though, so keep a weather eye on the long-term forecast while planning your woodsy getaway.

Remember, this as-yet thoroughly rural area is still relatively new to the tourist trade, so you won't find quaint bed-and-breakfasts for miles around. Should you prefer a firm mattress, air-conditioning,

♦ *Pitch your tent in the shade of live oaks draped with Spanish moss at the* **Brazos Bend State Park** *(21901 FM–762; 979–553–5101). Then roam by flashlight with the park's naturalist on a nighttime "owl prowl."*

♦ *Spend the morning on a camera safari in search of native birds or butterflies; then tour a spread of living Texas history at the* **George Ranch Historical Park** *(10215 FM–762; 281–545–9212), complete with a cowboy luncheon at the* **Dinner Belle Café.**

♦ *Stroll along the shady* **Creekfield Lake Nature Trail.** *Afterward take a peek at heavenly bodies through the 36-inch research telescope housed in the "Big Dome" of the* **George Observatory** *(21901 FM–762; 979–553–3400 or 713–639–4629) within the park.*

♦ *Hike the* **40 Acre Lake Loop Trail** *with binoculars to practice your birding skills, and admire the sweeping lake view from the five-story observation tower. Then angle your way into each other's hearts from the lake's* **Fishing Pier.**

and a roof over your heads to sleeping *au naturel*, there are a few budget motels in the nearby towns of Richmond and Rosenberg to choose from: The **Sundowner Motor Inn** (28382 Southwest Freeway; 281–342–6000; $39.95), the **Comfort Inn** (3555 Highway 36 South; 281–342–3700; $64), and the **Days Inn** (26010 Southwest Freeway; 281–342–6671; $54) are clean and reasonably priced alternatives to camping out.

DAY ONE: afternoon

Load up your camping gear and head out of Houston ahead of rush-hour traffic. Take US–59 South to the Crabb River Road/FM–2759 exit. (If you're new to these parts, note that "FM" stands for "farm to market" roads.) Turn left (east) onto FM–2759 and go about 2½ miles. Continue through the intersection where the road name changes to FM–762 (south). Follow the brown state-park signs for about 16 miles; you'll find **Brazos Bend State Park** (21901 FM–762; 979–553–5101; $3.00 admission fee) on the left.

Take advantage of the remaining daylight to pick the perfect campsite, pitch your tent, and settle in for the weekend. You'll find water, a tent pad, a barbecue grill and fire ring, a table, and a lantern holder at each of the park's well-equipped individual camping sites, along with clean rest rooms and hot showers at each camping area. If you forgot anything—and isn't there always something?—the **Visitors' Center Gift Shop**, operated by the park's volunteer organization, helpfully stocks snacks, drinks, ice, and firewood.

DAY ONE: evening

DINNER

Fire up that grill and prepare for your first outdoor feast. May we recommend a chilled bottle of sparkling cider—no alcohol in the park, darlings—while you wait for the charcoal to glow? Delve into your supply chest and pull out a pair of prime steaks, perhaps, and foil wrap some spuds to cook in the coals. Of course you remembered marshmallows to toast afterward, such gooey, fluffy fun to pop into your lover's mouth.

After dinner spritz on a little bug spray, grab your flashlights, and head out for an "owl prowl" evening hike with the park's naturalist, David Heinicke (call in advance for reservations and times; 979–553–5124). Life in this almost 5,000-acre park is very different after dark: You'll be amazed at the variety of nocturnal wildlife to see and hear, including great horned owls and barred owls, of course. These gentle treks cover between 1 and 2 miles of trail, usually lasting one and a half to two hours.

The embers of your fire may still be glowing late tonight as you lean back to marvel at the stars. You'll sleep warmly and well, snuggled into each other's arms, deep in your double sleeping bag.

DAY TWO: morning

BREAKFAST

Isn't it astonishing how fresh air inspires your appetites? Rise with the sun this morning, stoke the fire, and get that coffee started. Rustle up scrambled eggs in a cast-iron skillet, roll up a steaming corn tortilla or two, and your day is well under way.

This morning we recommend you two contemplate the birds and the bees, er, make that the butterflies, for loving inspiration. Some 270 species of birds can be spotted within the Brazos Bend environs—that's almost half the birds that fly Texas skies—as well as forty different kinds of native and migratory butterflies.

Guided birding hikes for beginners start every Saturday morning at 9:00 A.M. sharp. Bring your binoculars, sunscreen, and camera to the meeting place at the **40 Acre Lake** rest rooms. In addition to a dazzling array of feathered friends, you may also have a chance to see and photograph white-tailed deer, alligators, or even an elusive bobcat if you're very, very lucky.

The gentle jeweled butterflies are best seen in spring and summer. Monarchs and swallowtails gather round the special garden planted to attract them at the **Visitors' Center,** or you can join an early-morning butterfly hike with naturalist P. D. Hulce (contact him in advance by e-mail at pdhulce@io.com). The annual butterfly count in late June, for example, departs at 7:30 A.M. from the 40 Acre Lake parking lot.

DAY TWO: afternoon

This afternoon you'll leave the park to explore the historic environs of the **George Ranch Historical Park** (10215 FM–762; 281–545–9212), just down the road from Brazos Bend State Park. This outdoor museum of Texas history lies at the heart of a 23,000-acre working cattle ranch, the fruit of four frontier generations' labor and love.

LUNCH

First, take a break from your own camp cooking for lunch at the ranch's **Dinner Belle Café.** Here you'll find inexpensive, hearty options like hamburgers and barbecue.

After lunch stroll or hop a tram to explore the ranch's interpretive exhibits and demonstrations by costumed performers, divided by era into three sections. In the 1830s area you'll find the picturesque dogtrot cabin and stock farm of the first pioneers; the 1890s area boasts a Victorian mansion, a blacksmith shop, and a cowboy camp; and the 1930s area includes the George Ranch house, outbuildings, and cattle-working demonstrations. (Don't miss the enormous Jones treehouse!)

Before you leave stop by the **Dry Creek General Store** in the ranch's visitor center. Here you'll find a variety of historical books, old-fashioned candies, and other souvenirs, and also the stirring story on videotape of the ranch's founding pioneer couple, Henry and Nancy Jones, whose descendants built the cattle empire you've toured today.

That Western State of Mind

Prepare yourselves for the romance of the wild, wild West with an immersion in Texas author Larry McMurtry's sagas of **Lonesome Dove.** *The original Pulitzer Prize–winning novel to wear the title, and the resulting blockbuster miniseries starring Tommy Lee Jones and Robert Duvall, are the pick of the litter of later prequels and sequels, either on video or in print. The finely drawn portrayals of frontier life and love are engrossing and sometimes violent, but keep a cowboy bandanna handy for the tragic love stories of McCrae and Clara, and Call and Maggie.*

DAY TWO: evening

After an early supper round your campfire, hike down the quiet **Creekfield Lake Nature Trail** to find the **George Observatory** (21901 FM–762 Road; 979–553–3400 or 713–639–4629), a satellite facility of the Houston Museum of Natural Science. Passes to use its ten-ton, 36-inch research telescope are $2.00 per person and are allocated only on Saturday starting at 5:00 P.M. on a first-come, first-served basis. Far from the white glare of Houston's urban sprawl, you two will see stars like never before— and planets and nebulae, too. Trace the outline of your birth signs or simply marvel at the heavenly glory seen so close.

After taking your turns at the telescope, you can spread a blanket on the grass and keep an eye on the Milky Way through your binoculars, or you can head back to your campsite for a non-alcoholic nightcap followed by naturally sweet dreams.

DAY THREE: morning

After breakfast, gear up for a farewell hike through the park. There are 22 miles of marked nature trails to choose from; our favorite is the **40 Acre Lake Loop.** You'll have plenty of opportunities to practice your newly fledged songbird sighting skills along the levee between 40 Acre Lake and marshy Pilant Lake, and the occasional 'gator may cross your path. (Give these toothy behemoths a wide berth, and, like the other wild creatures you've encountered in the park, refrain from feeding them!)

When you get to the five-story observation tower, be sure to climb up for a spectacular view over the waters. It's a great place for photographs and, if you get there early enough, perfect for a private display of affection.

FOR MORE ROMANCE

If you'd like to extend your wildlife getaway just a bit longer, the fishing pier at 40 Acre Lake you hiked past provides prime angling for perch, crappie, catfish, and bass. You'll need your own tackle, a Texas freshwater fishing license, and your bait of choice (you can buy worms at the store just outside the park). There's no better way to wind up your weekend than with a couple of trophy fish crisping in your skillet. The park gates stay open long after dark (until 10:00 P.M.), so put off returning to city life as long as you can.

Sun, Sand, and Sea

☆On the Boardwalk

KEMAH

ALFWAY BETWEEN HOUSTON AND GALVESTON, the shores of Clear Lake (which is neither clear nor a lake, but actually a narrow saltwater bay) are chock-full of fun and romantic things to do and see, from sleek yachts to Ferris wheels to space shuttles at the NASA Space Center. Our first itinerary introduces you to the Clear Lake community of Kemah and its sweetly old-fashioned waterfront Boardwalk, complete with an eye-popping aquarium, seafood restaurants, a shopping village, and a miniature amusement park.

PRACTICAL NOTES: The best times to spend along Clear Lake include the fireworks displays at the Fourth of July and the **Harbor Parade of Lights** at Christmastime, when the narrow channel comes alive with a festively decorated fleet. If you're interested in one of these Clear Lake "prime times," do be sure to book your trip well in advance and ask your innkeeper about the range of special activities and events.

DAY ONE: afternoon

Driving south from Houston on the Gulf Freeway (Interstate 45), exit FM–518 and head east. (Note that "FM" stands for "farm to market" road.) Only a mile and a half east of the freeway, you'll find yourselves magically transported to the old-timey Main Street of little League City, shaded by one-hundred-year-old oak trees. Look for the cluster of brightly colored cottage shops on the right, clearly marked as **Founder's Square**. This is a great place to get out and

*R*om*a*n*c*e
AT A GLANCE

◆ On your way to Kemah, stop by historic League City for a trip back in time; browse the wares in quaint cottages at **Founder's Square** and pack a picnic lunch or snack from the **South Shore Tea Room** (501 East Main Street; 281–332–4069) to **League Park** or **Helen's Garden.**

◆ Even landlubbers will feel like Nantucket whalers while staying at the handsome **Captain's Quarters** (701 Bay Avenue; 281–334–4141) on the Kemah bayfront. After admiring the view from the widow's walk, you'll toast each other with exotic beers and dine heartily on German-style goodies at the **What's Cookin** restaurant (930 FM–518; 281–334–3610). When the band strikes up, dance to live music under the stars.

◆ Spend the morning shopping the quaint stores of Kemah's back streets; then lunch al fresco on the neighborhood's best barbecue at **T-Bone Tom's** (707 Highway 146; 281–334–2133).

◆ Explore the **Kemah Boardwalk**—without parking hassles!—this afternoon. Play games on the midway and footsie on the Ferris wheel. Then dine in fishy splendor at **The Aquarium** (11 Kemah Waterfront Street; 281–334–9010), the Boardwalk's flashiest restaurant.

◆ Wind up your weekend on the water with a short cruise of Clear Lake on the **Kemah Baywatch** tour boat (thirty-minute narrated tours, $6.00 per person; 713–477–1116).

stretch your legs and do some gift shopping. You'll find an eclectic jumble of curios, candles, cards, and antiques at **Gifts of the Heart** (501 East Main Street; 281–554–4554), **Nana's Attic** (501 East Main Street; 281–554–8199), and **Old Impressions/Teddy & Friends** (501 East Main Street; 281–338–4438).

If you're in the mood for a late lunch or mid-afternoon snack, pick up a pair of sandwiches at the **South Shore Tea Room** (501 East Main Street; 281–332–4069) in Founder's Square; then stroll across Main Street to **League Park,** which at one time was the site of this town's train depot. The picturesque gazebo makes a great background for photographs, and you can feed crumbs to the golden koi swimming in the pond. Just past Founder's Square is **Helen's Garden,** a pretty two-acre park abloom with local flowering plants, trees, and shrubs: It's another great spot for an impromptu picnic.

DAY ONE: evening

Now continue east toward Kemah along FM–518. (Be sure to stay on 518 by bearing right where the road forks into FM–2094.) Turn left (north) onto Highway 146 and then, almost immediately, turn right onto Seventh Street. This street ends—breathtakingly—at the shores of Galveston Bay, and you'll discover your home for the weekend on the right. The **Captain's Quarters** (701 Bay Avenue; 281–334–4141; $40 to $140) will remind you of a New England whaler's home, standing foursquare and proud on the waterfront. Of the six guest rooms named for famous sailing ships and space shuttles, our favorite is called the *Constitution*, which boasts a spectacular front view of the bay, a king-size antique bed, and a fireplace.

After you've unpacked, climb the stairs to the widow's walk atop the house for a gorgeous 360-degree view of Galveston Bay and Clear Lake. This spot is said to be the highest point in Kemah and is certainly one of the best places we know for a passionate embrace.

DINNER

Tonight you'll feast in true Teutonic fashion at the **What's Cookin** restaurant (930 FM–518; 281–334–3610; moderate), just up the same road you traveled in on. Watch for the restaurant's large roadside sign and then turn right into a lovely pecan grove. The shady patio is wonderful in warm weather, and a great starting point to explore the cafe's extensive roster of domestic and imported beers. (You can even join their Around the World in 80 Beers club; if you sample eighty different beers—over several visits, we hasten to add—you'll be rewarded with your own monogrammed beer mugs or matching T-shirts.)

House specialties here include generous servings of authentic wienerschnitzel, jaegershnitzel, and kassler rippchen, but don't worry about that Germanic calorie load. Once the weekend's band starts up on the outdoor stage, you'll dance them all off, perhaps while continuing to whittle away at the beer list.

DAY TWO: morning

After breakfasting in the antiques-filled formal dining room of the Captain's Quarters, you'll be well fortified for a morning of shopping along the quaint back streets of Kemah. All the stores and shops are conveniently within walking distance, so leave your car where it is and stroll, hand in hand.

Working your way north along Kipp Avenue toward the Boardwalk, you'll find the eclectic **Goin' South** at the corner of Kipp and Sixth, sporting a patio full of Mexican ceramics out front and a collection of Southwestern textiles and gourmet goodies indoors. Turn left on Sixth Street to find nautically themed clothing and sterling silver jewelry at **Carol & Co.** (603 Sixth Street; 281–334–2523), housed in a hundred-year-old cottage painted pea green. Tempt each other with tastes of the divine Boardwalk Fudge found at the **Eg-Quisite Egg Shell Shoppe** (605 Sixth Street; 281–538–4165) next door. Turn north again on Bradford and check out a variety of craftwork at the **Eagle's Nest Gallery** (511 Bradford Avenue; 281–538–1606). Then make your feet happy at **Birkenstocks & Boat Shoes** (409 Bradford Avenue; 281–535–2221), which, as its name promises, sells everything from sandals to Sperrys.

DAY TWO: afternoon

LUNCH

 From Bradford Avenue wander a block west along Seventh Street to find **T-Bone Tom's** (707 Highway 146; 281–334–2133; inexpensive) just in time for lunch. Not only does this friendly, funky combination restaurant and meat market boast some great Texas-style barbecue, their enormous chicken-fried steaks are pretty darned good, too. Even better, there's a shady patio out back with wooden picnic tables where you can take a load off. Aaah, that's more like it, isn't it?

Enjoy the relative peace and quiet at Tom's, because your next stop is the **Kemah Boardwalk,** one of the most popular attractions in the Houston metroplex. This fourteen-acre waterfront entertainment complex boasts theme restaurants, upscale souvenir shops, and even an amusement park. It's squeaky clean, immaculately landscaped, and stitched together by broad pedestrian avenues and a small-gauge train. Some locals sniff that it's too Disney-esque, but visitors return time and again to spend the day playing . . . some two million tourists a year, at last count.

You lucky things are already way ahead of the game, as you won't have to fuss with parking. Just stroll along and enjoy the sights. You'll find plenty more souvenirs, if you're not loaded down already, at **The Shops at Kemah** across from the Tex-Mex–themed **Cadillac Bar** (7 Kemah Waterfront Street; 281–334–9049). Should you weary, choose any one of the waterfront establishments for an afternoon cocktail—something tropical, with a paper parasol, perhaps.

As the afternoon wanes, try the fun and games of the amusement park. Recapture childhood bliss, feeding one another sweet tufts of cotton candy. Impress your lover with your athletic prowess at one of the midway's games of chance; no one can ever have too many silly stuffed animals.

Or maybe you'd prefer to spend the afternoon on ice. What twosome activity better combines glittery, skintight costumes, graceful movements to beautiful music, and mandatory hand-holding than ice skating? In the oppressive heat of a Texas summer, an afternoon of figure skating adds cool romance to your weekend's revels. You can lace up your boots and cut some figure eights on 50,000 square feet of ice at the **Texas Ice Stadium** (18150 Gulf Freeway, Friendswood; 281–486–7979).

DAY TWO: evening

Toward sundown get in line for the Ferris wheel. The view from the top is stunning, out over the sparkling bay. With luck your car will stop at the very top, long enough to get an eyeful of the view; then make out like teenagers, with the breeze ruffling your hair.

DINNER

Back on the ground again, wander over to **The Aquarium** (11 Kemah Waterfront Street; 281–334–9010; expensive). This is the crown jewel of all the themed restaurants on the Boardwalk; the "wow" factor is worth the wait you may have to endure on weekends. But who's in a hurry tonight? Put your name on the list and settle down together with a peachy frozen Bellini in the palapa-roofed bar on the ground floor, open to the Gulf breezes. Watch the children—and a few frivolous adults—playing in the spotlighted sidewalk fountains, which gush like Old Faithful at timed intervals.

Inside the restaurant a spiral staircase leads you to the second-story dining room, wrapping its way around a three-and-a-half story cylindrical tank containing 15,000 gallons of clear blue water and hundreds of tropical fish. The dining area centers on an even more astonishing sight: a complete reef structure in a 50,000-gallon tank, viewable from floor to ceiling through walls of thick plate acrylic. Skates and sharks and speckled trout sail by in apparent harmony, aloof to the diners and unruffled by the fate of their brethren on the plates.

Start with one of the generous appetizers, say, the imaginative lime-grilled chicken lettuce wraps stuffed with sprouts, sesame noodles, and peanuts or try the rich, caramel-colored lobster bisque. Then focus your attention on the big seafood platters, broiled or fried. And definitely don't skip dessert; the concoctions here are both showy and tasty. Indulge yourselves in the toasted almond and chocolate truffle cake or the sexy passion fruit crème brûlée.

After dinner you'll enjoy the breezy, moonlit walk back to your inn, only 5 blocks south along Kipp Avenue. Sit for a while by the bay on the inn's wide veranda, before climbing the stairs to your room. Tonight the gentle lapping of the waves will lull you—almost immediately—to sleep.

DAY THREE: morning

BREAKFAST

This morning you'll wake to the laughing of gulls floating by on bay breezes. Lounge late abed, if you like, before joining your fellow guests for breakfast in the formal dining room. Take your coffee out to the veranda and share the Sunday newspaper.

Afterward you can wind up your weekend on the water with a short cruise of Clear Lake. Weather permitting, the **Kemah Baywatch** tour boat (thirty-minute narrated tours are $6.00 per person;

713–477–1116) departs from the Kemah Boardwalk pier behind the Flying Dutchman restaurant between 1:00 and 6:00 P.M. on Sunday afternoons. This spiffy 36-foot boat, which looks something like a San Francisco trolley car, carries thirty-five passengers up the Clear Lake Channel and into Clear Lake. You can admire the view from inside in air-conditioned comfort or step outside to catch some of the sun's rays. After all, what's sexier than that healthy, windblown glow?

Backwater Bliss

The Laid-Back Side of Kemah and Seabrook

SSSH, DON'T TELL ANYONE, but there's more to Kemah than that famous Boardwalk. In this itinerary we'll show you some surprisingly quiet spots to get away from it all: sheltering in a secluded garden, sailing over wind-ruffled water, or slipping through the rustling grasses of a nature preserve. Follow our cues to escape the clamor and, with art and love and creativity, achieve a Zen-like inner peace with the world and each other.

PRACTICAL NOTES: Before you book your trip, contact Barney & Beverly Goodman (281–992–5817, or e-mail bgoodman@pdq.net) to find out who's playing on the back deck in their bimonthly series of **Texas Nights House Concerts.**

Schedule individual rock-carving sessions with the innkeepers/artists for your mutual convenience when you make your reservations at the **Sculpture Garden Tranquil Bed N Breakfast.**

DAY ONE: afternoon

The **Sculpture Garden Tranquil Bed N Breakfast** (710 Bradford Avenue; 281–334–2517; $95) is a very special place, as you'll realize the moment you cross the threshold. Your hosts are award-winning artists Danny and Julie Meeks, and the enchanting garden behind their home is filled with tinkling fountains, grinning gargoyles, and other playful creatures, all sprung from their imaginations and carved from ancient lava rock. Overhead, flocks of bright-green wild

Romance AT A GLANCE

♦ Hide away in a field of dreams at the **Sculpture Garden Tranquil Bed N Breakfast** (710 Bradford Avenue; 281–334–2517).

♦ Pick a vessel for a romantic dinner cruise across the calm waters of Clear Lake. Dine and dance aboard a motorized yacht from **Star Fleet Entertainment Yachts** (South Shore Harbor Marina at 2400 South Shore Boulevard; 713–334–4692) or slip away on the **Lady Christina,** a 70-foot luxury sailing vessel, through Majestic Ventures (H Dock at Kemah Harbor Marina; 281–334–5325).

♦ Borrow your innkeepers' golf cart and putter over to the **Kemah Bay Café** (310 Texas Avenue; 281–334–6163) for a hearty waterside breakfast. Then sculpt your morning away.

♦ Lunch is at a local favorite called **Tookie's Restaurant** (1202 Bayport Boulevard; 281–474–3444) in Seabrook; afterward you can play hooky with a cold beer at pretty-in-pink **Maribelle's** (305 Bath Street; 281–474–9919) under the bridge.

♦ Spend a laid-back evening with backyard barbecue and outstanding acoustic music at the **Texas Nights House Concert** series, hosted by Barney & Beverly Goodman (703 Ferndale Court, Friendswood; 281–992–5817, or e-mail bgoodman@pdq.net).

♦ Commune with nature at the nearby **Armand Bayou Nature Center** (8500 Bay Area Boulevard, Pasadena; 281–474–2551), choosing a program of hiking, canoeing, or just hanging out.

parrots—native to this part of the Texas Gulf Coast—flash squawking through the trees.

Three small cottages are ranged about, each very comfortable and complete with well-equipped kitchens. (Note that the "N" in the Sculpture Garden Tranquil Bed N Breakfast stands for "No breakfast," meaning that the Meeks provide you with a coffeemaker, coffee, and fresh pastries. Pack in your own "extra" gourmet goodies as you see fit.)

At the Sculpture Garden Tranquil Bed N Breakfast, you'll have a unique opportunity to co-create a work of art in surprisingly lightweight lava rock, an everlasting memento of this magical weekend. In individualized classes available only to guests, the Meeks will guide you through the easy steps (really!) to create a sculpture or waterfall. Working together, the two of you can finish your creation this weekend. Tour the garden for inspiration; then get started this afternoon roughing out your masterpiece.

DAY ONE: evening

DINNER

Just before the sun touches the yardarm, so to speak, we recommend you take a break from your carving and consider a sunset dinner cruise, one of the unique perks of calm Clear Lake. **Star Fleet Entertainment Yachts** (South Shore Harbor Marina at 2400 South Shore Boulevard; 713–334–4692) offers dinner-dance cruises on 100- or 150-passenger power yachts for around $70 per couple. Or splurge on an elegant dinner cruise ($120 to $140 per couple) aboard the *Lady Christina,* a 70-foot luxury sailing vessel, through Majestic Ventures (H Dock at Kemah Harbor Marina; 281–334–5325). Dinner-cruise schedules are variable, and reservations are required for either adventure; and, if you go the sailing route, do remember to wear soft-soled shoes.

DAY TWO: morning

BREAKFAST

You'll wake this morning to joyful parrot calls and the soothing sound of splashing water from a dozen fountains. Before returning to your art, rustle up some coffee and croissants in your cottage kitchen or borrow the Meeks' golf cart and putter over to the **Kemah Bay Café** (310 Texas Avenue; 281–334–6163; inexpensive) for one of the best breakfasts around. Look for the blue-and-white lighthouse on the west side of the Kemah Harbor Marina; you can't miss it. The cafe's specialty is called Mess in a Pan, which, despite its unlovely name, is a delicious egg-free scramble of shaved rib-eye steak, tomatoes, peppers, and hash browns topped with cheddar cheese.

Spend your morning perfecting your sculpture.

DAY TWO: afternoon

LUNCH

For lunch we suggest a local favorite called **Tookie's Restaurant** (1202 Bayport Boulevard; 281–474–3444). It's a short but scenic drive north along Highway 146 and across the bridge to Seabrook; you'll easily find Tookie's on the right. Here, the handmade hamburgers are excellent; finish out your order with crisp, golden onion rings and a big cherry Coke.

No matter how eager you are to return to your art, if the afternoon is sunny and fine, it will be hard to resist the temptation to play a little hooky or, if you're done carving, skip out with a clear conscience. The perfect place to while away your afternoon is **Maribelle's** (305 Bath Street; 281–474–9919), a rambling, unexpectedly pink-painted building tucked under the Seabrook bridge. Headed back south toward Kemah, turn off just before the bridge on Shipyard Drive and wend your way toward it. It's a funky, comfortable place to sip a cold, long-neck beer and play your favorite tunes on the jukebox. Shoot some pool or sit out on the patio and watch the ship traffic go by.

DAY TWO: evening

DINNER

Your evening's entertainment is an unbeatable combination of backyard barbecue and outstanding acoustic music at the **Texas Nights House Concert** series, hosted by Barney & Beverly Goodman (703 Ferndale Court, Friendswood; 281–992–5817, or e-mail bgoodman@pdq.net). To get there you'll return to I–45 and go north to the FM–2351 exit; the Goodmans will give you more specific directions when you make your reservations.

Now why would anyone turn their private home into a concert hall for anywhere from fifty to one hundred fans? As the Goodmans explain, it's purely for the love of the music. The cover charge is minimal, and it all goes to the artists. Most folks bring a covered dish, so you can pick something up at **T-Bone Tom's** (707 Highway 146; 281–334–2133), if you like.

It's a music-lover's heaven out there in the sweet evening air, like a great folk-music club without the funk. You and your lover will settle back into your lawn chairs on the grass among a quiet, deeply appreciative crowd and thank your lucky stars—twinkling right overhead—for this weekend.

DAY THREE: morning

BREAKFAST

This morning rise bright and early to commune with nature at the nearby **Armand Bayou Nature Center** (8500 Bay Area Boulevard, Pasadena; 281–474–2551). It's a spectacular 2,500-acre stretch of pristine wilderness, encompassing woodlands, prairie, and estuarine ecosystems complete with the feathered, scaled, and furred denizens you'd never dream of seeing so close to civilization. The center offers regular programs of hikes, cruises, and canoe trips on Sunday mornings, often combined with a light continental breakfast, lasting anywhere from two to four hours. (Call in advance for schedule information.)

One popular Sunday option is a ride on a pontoon boat called the *Bayou Ranger*, followed by a hike along the little-visited West Bank of the bayou. Well-marked trails elsewhere in the preserve beckon the more independent-minded folks, and there are plenty of secluded spots to appreciate each other, as well as the flora and fauna. If you're not on one of the breakfast jaunts, pack your own nibbles, along with sensible shoes, bug repellent, and binoculars.

FOR MORE ROMANCE

Ever wonder what pioneer life was really like in the wild, wild West? Then stick around the Armand Bayou Nature Center for the afternoon demonstrations held most Sundays from 1:00 to 4:00 P.M. These range from frontier chores like butter, cheese, or rope making, cooking on a wood stove, or basic blacksmithing at the Jimmy Martyn Farm Site, to nature lectures at the educational center. Again, it's best to double-check the schedule with an advance phone call to (281) 474–2551.

Maybe you two would like to make an entirely different sort of music together: warbling love songs to one another before a roomful of strangers, perhaps? If so, check into the schedule for **Vicki's Celebrations Karaoke,** a traveling circus of music and microphones held at various venues in the Clear Lake area, including **The Aquarium** (11 Kemah Waterfront Street; 281–334–9010) and **Studio 54 Cafe** (3329 East Nasa Road 1; 281–326–2758). Vicki promises that your special song will be in her play list; from the macarena to Megadeath, she says, her tunes are "sure to match anyone's taste— or lack of it." Don't be shy; be silly together!

Clear Sailing on Clear Lake

HE CLEAR LAKE AREA boasts nineteen marinas with more than 7,000 boat slips, which all adds up to the third-largest concentration of sailboats and powerboats in North America. In this itinerary you'll take to the salt waves aboard a sailing or power yacht, and even aboard a floating bar, for a nautical happy hour. To liven things up on land, there's gambling at the nearby Gulf Greyhound Park and dancing on the shore by moonlight. By day or by night, at sea or ashore, Clear Lake can be your lovers' playground.

PRACTICAL NOTES: A very special time to visit the Johnson Space Center is during the **Ballunar Lift-Off Festival** (www.ballu narfestival.com) every August. This magical celebration of flight ranges from hot-air balloons to the space shuttles, with daring sky divers sprinkled in between. Or for a touch of comic relief, try the Gulf Greyhound Park during its January **Weiner Dog Nationals,** as dozens of dachshunds compete merrily for prizes.

DAY ONE: afternoon

Slip away from the city early this afternoon, if you can, to cleverly escape the traffic and catch the sunset from the deck at **Lance's Turtle Club** (2613½ NASA Road 1; 281–326–7613). Take the Gulf Freeway (Interstate 45) south to NASA Road 1 and turn east, toward the Gulf. The party starts every Friday afternoon at this laid-back

Romance

AT A GLANCE

◆ Kick off your weekend with cocktails afloat at **Lance's Turtle Club** (2613½ NASA Road 1; 281–326–7613); then snuggle into your waterside cottage at the **Beacon Hill Guest House Bed and Breakfast** (3705 NASA Road 1; 281–326–7643).

◆ Dine al fresco in the Roman gardens at the **Villa Capri** Italian restaurant (3713 NASA Road 1; 281–326–2373). Then go dancing at the **Seabrook Beach Club** (3345 NASA Road 1; 281–326–5819), at its patio party under the stars.

◆ Spend the day at sea, either as swabbie sailing students or pampered charter guests aboard the yachts of **Gateway Charters and Sailing School** (585 Bradford, Kemah Marina; 281–334–4606) or **Hidden Harbor Yacht Charter & Sales** (Pier 21, Kemah Marina; 281–334–2633).

◆ Tonight you two will "go to the dogs" for dinner and a bit of betting at the **Gulf Greyhound Park** in nearby La Marque (I–45 South, exit 15, La Marque; 800–ASK–2–WIN). Highrollers and novices alike can play the puppies in air-conditioned comfort and go home winners.

◆ After a sea captain's breakfast spread at the **Seabrook Classic Café** (2511 NASA Road 1 #A; 281–326–1512), you'll enjoy a thrilling peek behind the scenes at the Johnson Space Center's visitor center, **Space Center Houston** (1601 NASA Road 1; 281–244–2100). Touch a moon rock or embrace with Earth rising over your lover's shoulder; it's all out of this world.

floating bar; try for a seat at the rough wooden picnic tables on the top deck for a spectacular view over the water. You'll feel your week's worth of tension melting away within moments as you lazily wait for the sunset.

DAY ONE: evening

Now find your way back just a few blocks west on NASA Road 1 to the **Beacon Hill Guest House Bed and Breakfast** (3705 NASA Road 1; 281–326–7643; $75 to $105). Your cozy yellow cottage, called the Studio, is complete with cathedral ceiling and kitchenette and is only steps away from the shore of Clear Lake. (We also like the Sterling Suite for its king-size bed and hot tub.) Take a moment before dinner to stroll out to the end of Beacon Hill's pier and steal kisses, backlit by the twinkling lights of boats headed for their snug harbors.

DINNER

Dinner tonight is practically next door to your inn at the rambling **Villa Capri** Italian restaurant (3713 NASA Road 1; 281–326–2373; moderate). The menu combines fresh seafood with accents of southern Italian pasta, pretty standard stuff—but, oh, the ambience is tailor-made for lovestruck couples like you. Ask for a candlelit table outside on the patio, overlooking the formal gardens and the water. You may even see a blissfully newlywed couple departing by boat from the restaurant's dock.

Do you crave a little more excitement or feel a guilty need to work off that ravioli? Then you can dance under the stars at the lively **Seabrook Beach Club** (3345 NASA Road 1; 281–326–5819) just down the road, which features live music every weekend for its "party on the patio." There's just something about jiving to golden oldies by moonlight that will set your hearts beating in tune.

DAY TWO: morning

After breakfast at your inn, put on your sailing shoes for a day on the water, departing from the nearby **Kemah Marina.** Follow NASA Road 1 east to Highway 146; then turn south and cross the bridge to Kemah. Active do-it-yourselfers can arrange full-day sailing lessons from **Gateway Charters and Sailing School** (585 Bradford, Kemah Marina; 281–334–4606) or **Hidden Harbor Yacht Charter & Sales** (Pier 21, Kemah Marina; 281–334–2633), or you can simply charter a boat and crew to float you along effortlessly.

DAY TWO: afternoon

LUNCH

Lunch today is aboard your sailboat, thoughtfully packed for you by the charter company. Supplement your sustenance with kisses and hugs; no one can live on bread alone, you know. By now you're both proficient sailors, skimming the shallow waves all afternoon. You did bring a camera, didn't you? Be sure to take souvenir photographs of the two of you, handsomely burnished by the sun and breeze.

After you've docked and gotten your land legs back, you can return to your inn for a splash in the hot tub and a leisurely nap. Don't worry; there's plenty of time for relaxation before tonight's fun and games.

DAY TWO: evening

DINNER

This evening you'll enjoy something completely different: dinner livened by a spot of genteel gambling at the **Gulf Greyhound Park** in nearby La Marque (I–45 South, exit 15, La Marque; 800–ASK–2–WIN). This 110-acre greyhound-racing complex is one of the largest, cleanest, and most comfortable in the world; even the greyhounds live the life of Riley here: The eighteen kennels boast hot and cold running water, whirlpools, central heat and air-conditioning, and even smoke alarms.

Reserve two seats in the **Horizon Clubhouse** for dinner. You'll get a good meal of steaks or seafood at a reasonable price, plus a bird's-eye view of the track action through the floor-to-ceiling windows as well as close-ups from the clever little color television monitor right at your table.

The evening performance kicks off at 7:30 P.M., and the action is fast and furious, so if you're unsure how to bet, study the monitor for instructions or look for one of the many helpful track associates. Pari-mutuel betting can be great fun, and this track has paid out more than half a billion dollars to other lucky winners—why not you? By the end of the evening, you'll be boxing those quinielas with ease. Use your winnings to buy each other funny souvenirs at one of the track's three gift shops—or maybe take your windfall and use it to adopt a greyhound of your own. Should you two fall in love with these well-trained, elegant beasts and desire one for your own castle, check into the adoption program for retired racers sponsored by the **Gulf Greyhound Park.** More than 1,000 greyhounds have been placed in loving homes under the auspices of this program, and many owners treat their beloved dogs to an annual reunion at the track.

DAY THREE: morning

BREAKFAST

 This morning you can enjoy a leisurely breakfast at your inn, or if you're feeling gregarious, drive just a few blocks west and rub shoulders with the local boating crowd at the **Seabrook Classic Café** (2511 NASA Road 1 #A; 281–326–1512; inexpensive). We're particularly fond of their pancakes; the omelets are excellent, too.

Then make sure you're wearing sturdy walking shoes for your morning tour of **Space Center Houston** (1601 NASA Road 1; 281–244–2100), conveniently located on the way home along NASA Road 1. If you ever thrilled to the words, "Houston, the Eagle has landed," you won't want to miss the tour of NASA's Johnson Space Center Mission Control Center, the heart of the manned space flight program. The beauty of this massive education and entertainment complex adjoining JSC is that all tours are self-guided, so you can decide exactly how much you'd like to see.

We recommend you allocate at least a half-day to land a shuttle or retrieve a satellite (through computer simulation, of course), ride the JSC tram tour, or take in an impressive IMAX film about the space program. Most romantic of all is the dimly lit gallery that offers you the same jaw-dropping view of Earth that astronauts saw from the Moon: a shadowy corner here makes for a marvelous spot to make out. Talk about "the mile high club"!

LUNCH

Come back to earth for a late lunch, Latin-style, at **Churrasco's** (1320 Bay Area Boulevard; 281–461–4100; moderate to expensive). You can't miss the black-and-white spotted-cow exterior just off the Gulf Freeway. Inside, the legendary Cordua brothers' menu is sure fire. Start with a pisco sour, a margarita-like drink made with fiery Peruvian brandy, and nibble on crisp slivers of plantain chips dunked in garlicky, addictive chimichurri sauce. Then feast your way through the pan-tropical spectrum of entrees. Choices include Gambas Encaramanoladas (colossal shrimp encrusted with yuca, black beans, and chorizo), Cerdo Relleno (roasted pork tenderloin rolled and filled with fresh corn and cheese pudding), and extraordinary Churrasco steak (succulent char-grilled beef tenderloin, butterflied and bathed in that same chimichurri sauce).

Galveston Island
ROMANCING THE STRAND

ALVESTON ISLAND MARKS THE STARTING POINT of the "Texas Riviera," the long crescent of Gulf Coast shoreline that stretches from Louisiana to Mexico. The island is situated less than an hour's drive south of Houston, but the other side of the causeway seems a world away, with much less traffic, far fewer people, and 32 miles of sunny beaches sprawled along the gentle Gulf of Mexico. Life here moves at a slower, more relaxed pace . . . on "island time."

Our first itinerary in the Galveston area recaptures the romantic history of Galveston Island, as it was before the tragic storm of 1900. Stroll the Strand—itself a National Historic Landmark—for shopping and dining, visit vintage Victorian homes and a classic sailing ship, and ride horse-drawn carriages.

PRACTICAL NOTES: Galveston's peak tourist season is summer, from Memorial Day to Labor Day, when it's the most visited resort area in Texas. Sure, Texas summers are sultry, but the island is always a few breezy degrees cooler than the mainland. After Labor Day the crowds melt away as if by magic. December brings **Dickens on the Strand** and the **Harbor Parade of Lights.** The island's biggest bacchanal, **Mardi Gras,** happens sometime between January and April, luring half a million visitors every year with parades, sexy costumes, bead throws, and fancy dress balls. Springtime, from March through May, offers some of the finest beach weather of the year. As the island gears up again for summer, you'll find street festivals and beach parties and home and garden tours as the oleanders—Galveston's official flower—come into bloom.

Romance AT A GLANCE

◆ Revel in the luxury of Galveston's most elegant hotel, the **Tremont House** (2300 Ship's Mechanic Row; 800–874–2300 or 409–763–0300), and dine à deux just around the corner at the incredibly romantic **Luigi's Ristorante Italiano** (2328 Strand; 409–763–6500).

◆ Breakfast Parisian style on the sunny, greenery-fringed patio of the **Phoenix Bakery & Coffee House** (220 Tremont Street; 409–763–4611). Ride in a horse-drawn carriage through the quaint Strand shopping district, then imagine yourselves in times gone by as you tour Galveston's grand historic homes: the **Moody Mansion** (2618 Broadway; 409–762–7668), the **Ashton Villa and Museum** (2328 Broadway; 409–762–3933), and the imposing **Bishop's Palace** (1402 Broadway; 409–762–2475).

◆ Choose from **Yaga's** "tropical cafe" (2314 Strand; 409–762–6676) or **The Strand Brewery** (101 Twenty-third Street; 409–763–4500) for a leisurely lunch, then set out hand in hand to explore the Strand, chock-a-block with shops, small galleries, and funky watering holes.

◆ Take a sunset stroll along the harbor front, then dine waterside at the **Fisherman's Wharf** restaurant (Pier 22 & Harborside Drive; 409–765–5708) in the shadow of the tall ship Elissa, moored at the **Texas Seaport Museum** at Pier 21 (Harborside Drive between Twenty-first and Twenty-second Streets; 409–763–1877).

◆ Bring your getaway weekend to a close in sunshine and salt air with a scenic boat tour of Galveston's Harbor on a 50-foot catamaran. The tour departs from **Pier 22 at Harborside** (409–765–1700 or 409–762–8815).

DAY ONE: evening

From Houston, take I–45 south to Galveston Island. The highway terminates at Galveston's tree-lined Broadway; from Broadway, turn left on Twenty-third Street into the Strand District. Turn left on Ship's Mechanic Row, also known simply as Mechanic Street, to find your destination: Galveston's most elegant hotel, the **Tremont House** (2300 Ship's Mechanic Row; 800–874–2300 or 409–763–0300; standard rooms $129 to $220, depending on the season; suites, $250 and up). Just around the corner from the bustling Strand's shops, galleries, and restaurants, the Tremont is set on a charming, quiet block of Ship's Mechanic Row.

The Tremont's crisp black-and-white color scheme is the perfect backdrop for your sybaritic getaway, from the marble tiles of the soaring four-story atrium, furnished with potted palms and white wicker armchairs, to the luxurious rooms graced with brass beds and Victorian-style armoires, 14-foot ceilings, and polished hardwood floors. Ask for the Tremont's "Romantic Rendezvous" package, and your room will be supplied with champagne, roses, and chocolate-dipped strawberries, plus trolley tickets and breakfast in bed.

DINNER

Stroll around the block to the Strand to dine at **Luigi's Ristorante Italiano** (2328 Strand; 409–763–6500; expensive; reservations recommended), one of the island's finest and most romantic restaurants. The high-ceilinged rooms of a turn-of-the-century bank have been transformed into an elegant Italian trattoria, with glowing peach walls and tall archways topped with graceful terra-cotta wine jars. A polished mahogany bar dominates the front room, paved with old-fashioned black-and-white tiles. Strains of operatic arias drift out to the street, along with the rich scents of garlic and olive oil. (This being laid-back Galveston, of course, you'll find your fellow diners' dress comfortably runs the gamut from glittery cocktail dresses to faded Polo shirts.)

Chef Luigi Ferré has a deft touch with pasta—like the Penne Rustico, with sausage, spinach, and mozzarella topped with zucchini strips and tomato-cream sauce—but his lamb and veal dishes should not be overlooked. Try the Agnello al Ferri, baby lamb chops marinated in red wine, balsamic vinegar, and olive oil, seasoned with rosemary, mint, and garlic, and seared to order; or the Vitello al Funghi, exceptionally tender sautéed veal scaloppine with a sun-dried tomato sauce and thick slabs of fresh porcini mushrooms. For dessert share a piece of the custardy-rich tiramisù, layered with ladyfingers soaked in Kahlua and Amaretto liqueurs, or try the Torta de Crostata al Lamponi, an almond-butter crust laced with sticky raspberry puree and topped with fresh raspberries.

Return to the Tremont's genteel **Toujouse Bar** in the atrium lobby for a nightcap. Settle into a wicker plantation chair to listen to live piano music or quiet jazz or slip away to the guests-only Rooftop Terrace for a stunning view of Galveston's harbor by moonlight. There's plenty of room for romance on this dimly lit and usually deserted piazza . . . need we say more?

DAY TWO: morning

BREAKFAST

 The sunny, greenery-fringed patio of the **Phoenix Bakery & Coffee House** (220 Tremont Street; 409–763–4611; inexpensive) makes a lovely spot for the two of you to enjoy a leisurely breakfast, and it's just around the corner from your hotel. Turn left on Ship's Mechanic and left again on Tremont Street. You'll see the lush green lawn and brick walls of the Phoenix on the right.

It's difficult to choose from all the tempting flaky pastries on display in the Phoenix's glass case, but the authentic New Orleans–style beignets, golden brown and dusted with confectioner's sugar, are devastating with a cup of rich, dark coffee. The mesquite-smoked salmon served with red onions and cream cheese atop a toasted bagel is also enticing.

After breakfast, stroll half a block north on the Strand, where your carriage awaits. There's no better way to tour this historic district than by **horse-drawn carriage,** the slow clip-clop of hooves echoing from the quaint high curbs and shady storefront canopies. A thirty-minute promenade costs about $20 for two; you can simply strike a deal with one of the drivers waiting along the Strand or make arrangements in advance by calling **Island Carriages** (409–765–6951) or **Seahorse Carriages** (409–925–3312).

At the end of the last century, Galveston's Strand was known as the "Wall Street of the Southwest," lined with buildings designed by the best and brightest architects of Victorian Galveston. Many of those nineteenth-century buildings still stand, having survived the destruction of the Great Storm of 1900 as well as the devastating fires that periodically swept downtown. These handsome buildings now house an intriguing collection of stores and galleries, so be sure to make note of the ones you'd like to explore later.

Strand sights include the former First National Bank Building, built in 1878 (corner of Strand and Twenty-second Street), sporting a frontispiece of white-painted, cast-iron Corinthian columns, now home to the **Galveston Arts Center,** the city's major public art gallery with regular exhibitions of photography, painting, and sculpture. And within the antebellum Hendley Buildings, built in 1859 of red brick trimmed in gray granite, you'll find the **Strand Visitors Center,** a valuable source of historic information, maps, and brochures, and the **Hendley Market,** which houses an eclectic collection of gift items, books, and toys.

Now that you two have mastered the general lay of the land in the Strand district, it's time to explore the nearby mansions of the turn-of-the-twentieth-century moguls who built this charming city. Galveston Island has more than 550 designated historical land-marks on the National Register of Historic Places and more than 1,500 restored historic homes. Three of the most impressive homes—mansions, really—have been lovingly restored, inside and out, and are open daily for public viewing. They are known as the "Broadway Beauties," as each faces onto Broadway, a busy but still lovely boulevard, its median thickly planted with oleander, live oak, and palm trees.

Your tour begins with the **Moody Mansion** (2618 Broadway; 409–762–7668). You can drive or walk from the Strand down Twenty-sixth Street or arrange with your carriage driver to drop you nearby. Allow approximately thirty minutes for a self-guided tour of the home.

This thirty-one-room Romanesque Revival mansion, built in 1895 of brick and limestone, was purchased for the bargain price of $20,000 after the Great Storm of 1900 by W. L. Moody, Jr., a scion of one of Galveston's most influential families. In addition to a financial empire in cotton and banking, Moody also owned the *Galveston News* and the American National Insurance Company, at present two of the largest employers on the island. Home to the Moody family for more than eighty years, the mansion's restoration began shortly after Hurricane Alicia in 1983.

A warm sense of family still pervades the Moody Mansion, as the original furnishings are all in place, right down to their wicker rocking chairs, fishing rods, and high-button shoes. You can easily picture yourselves as one of the hundred gowned and tuxedoed couples who danced at elder daughter Mary's oh-so-elegant debut party in 1911, while a full orchestra played in the conservatory.

Now stroll 3 blocks south along Broadway to find the **Ashton Villa and Museum** (2328 Broadway; 409–762–3933). Time your arrival to coincide with the guided tours that begin every hour on the hour.

One of the wealthiest businessmen in nineteenth-century Texas, James Moreau Brown, designed and built this Italianate villa in 1859, using bricks from his own brickyard. His is the only mansion on Broadway to survive both the Civil War and the Great Storm of 1900. This tour gives you a shivery insight into the devastation of the Great Storm, with a hair-raising program on the lethal hurricane and its aftermath. After the island's massive grade-raising project, the once-elevated main floor of the villa found itself at street level; between the house and the stables you can get a peek into an archaeological excavation into the pre-1900 levels underneath.

While it's an easy walk in fine weather, on inclement or hotter days you may wish to drive an additional 8 blocks south to the imposing **Bishop's Palace** (1402 Broadway; 409–762–2475). Guided tours begin every half hour and last approximately thirty-five minutes.

Walter Gresham, a Confederate colonel who later served as a U.S. congressman, completed his ornate mansion in 1893 at the then-staggering cost of $250,000. Gresham's neighbors called it a "castle"; it wasn't until the local Catholic diocese acquired it in 1923 that it came to be known as a "palace." The American Institute of Architecture has declared it an architectural masterpiece, ranking it as one of the top one hundred homes in the country.

Colonel Gresham was a fireplace collector. He searched the world for elaborate mantelpieces, and then had rooms designed to house them. The music room's mantelpiece is fashioned from onyx and silver, while the front ballroom's mantel won first prize at the Philadelphia World's Fair in 1876.

DAY TWO: afternoon

LUNCH

After all of this walking, you'll surely have worked up an appetite. You'll return to the Strand for a late lunch before enjoying a laid-back afternoon of strolling and shopping together.

Yaga's "tropical cafe" on the Strand (2314 Strand; 409–762–6676; inexpensive) is a casual, up-beat place to dine with a youthful crowd. You can't miss the hanging sign: a cartoon head sketched with Rastafarian dreadlocks. Sandwiches, salads, and juicy Yaga Burgers are constructed with fresh ingredients on a Caribbean theme, with a number of heart-healthy selections. Try to get a table for two at the front windows, which open directly onto the Strand's bustling sidewalk, for some great people watching. Be sure to ask for the specialty cocktail menu: Yaga's bar whips up excellent frozen tropical fruit drinks guaranteed to put you in a sensuous Caribbean frame of mind.

The patio of **The Strand Brewery** (101 Twenty-third Street; 409–763–4500; moderate), a block down Twenty-third Street from Yaga's, is another wonderful spot for lunch. This is Galveston's first microbrewery, producing colorfully named brews like the amber Great Storm Lager or the full-bodied, dark Brown Pelican. Individual pizzas are fired in a wood-burning oven: The roasted garlic with spinach, sun-dried tomatoes, and two kinds of cheese is popular, as is the Gulf shrimp pizza spiked with jalapeño peppers.

You two can spend this afternoon strolling the Strand, peeking into its assortment of shops; or, if you're feeling especially lazy, grab a couple of good books and curl up contentedly in side-by-side chaises on the Tremont House's sunny rooftop.

The best place on the island to find a good book is the independently owned **Midsummer Books** (2311 Ship's Mechanic Row; 409–765–5930). This cozy shop, across the street from the Tremont House hotel, is plentifully stocked with a carefully chosen selection of hardbacks and paperbacks, including a section on island history, architecture, flora, and fauna. Can't decide? Ask the genial owner, Jay Clements, for a recommendation. He and his wife are adventurous readers eager to share their favorites.

Sure, the Strand has its share of tacky trinkets and T-shirts. But look closely and you'll unearth treasures. Some Strand District shops worth seeing include **Su Casa Southwest Interiors** (2402 Strand; 409–763–2424), with its hand-carved and brightly painted Mexican furniture; be sure to check out the sorta-spooky Frida Kahlo room. At **Colonel Bubbie's** (2202 Strand; 409–762–7397), you'll feel like kids playing in grandma's attic. This eccentric ware-house is crammed with military surplus clothing, sailor's hats, pirate flags, ammunition bags, you name it. When entering, be care-ful not to let out the resident cats. Stop by **Two Friends Gallery** (2301 Strand; 409–765–7477) for whimsical art jewelry, glass, and ceramics created by artists near and far. Looking for love charms? Then don't miss the **Hendley Market** (2010 Strand; 409–762–2610) for an eclectic collection of antique books, voodoo dolls, charms and spells, Mexican santos, and, of course, the ever-popular giant rubber bugs.

DAY TWO: evening

Tonight you'll spend a relaxing evening on **Galveston's Harbor**, prettiest after sunset when lights from passing ships twinkle over the water. Harborside Drive is easy to find, running parallel to the Strand only 1 block to the north.

DINNER

Your dinner destination is conveniently next door to the Seaport Museum: the **Fisherman's Wharf** restaurant (Pier 22 and Harborside Drive; 409–765–5708; moderate). The best seats in the house are on the spacious wooden deck right on the water, with the *Elissa* rocking gently at her mooring alongside your table for two. Indulge yourselves in soft talk by torchlight and impeccably pre-pared fresh seafood, like Gulf snapper Pontchartrain, topped with crabmeat, or the waterfront favorite, fried jumbo shrimp. Don't miss the dreamy pecan and chocolate pie, served warm and topped with scoops of vanilla ice cream for dessert.

Have you two still got energy to burn? Head up Twenty-first Street to Postoffice to find **"21"** (2102 Postoffice; 409–762–2101). This Art Deco–inspired club has a speakeasy feel and a vivacious late-night crowd. The full-service bar offers twenty-one variations on the clas-sic martini, fifty different wines by the glass, and an assortment of cigars. Sink into an overstuffed sofa for an amorous tête-à-tête or hit the dance floor to live music on weekends.

DAY THREE: morning

This morning you've earned the luxury of breakfast in bed. Dial room service and order up croissants, fresh strawberries, and a steaming pot of coffee. Wrap yourselves in the Tremont's fluffy robes of thick white terry cloth and read the best bits of the Sunday newspaper aloud to each other.

After checkout you two can wind up your romantic weekend shipboard for a scenic **boat tour** of Galveston's harbor. Seduced by the sea breeze and sunshine, couples like you lean close at the railing. The 50-foot diesel-powered catamaran departs from Pier 22 at Harborside (409–765–1700 or 409–762–8815). Call ahead, as schedules and itineraries vary; you can generally choose from a dolphin-watch cruise or a narrated historical tour of the harbor.

FOR MORE ROMANCE

You'll both enjoy the small, charming **Texas Seaport Museum** at Pier 21 (Harborside Drive between Twenty-first and Twenty-second Streets; 409–763–1877). The star of the museum's collection is the tall ship *Elissa*, berthed just outside. Almost one hundred years after her 1877 christening, the iron barque *Elissa* was discovered in sadly reduced circumstances, smuggling Turkish cigarettes in the Mediterranean. A short film dramatizes her fairy-tale story of rescue and restoration to National Historic Landmark status.

Island Arts and Entertainment in the East End

HE EAST END OF THE ISLAND is Galveston's historic district. Prettily restored Victorian homes with brightly painted gingerbread trim line quiet residential streets shaded by live oaks and palm trees; some have been converted to cozy bed-and-breakfasts, like your romantic hideaway for this itinerary. Only a few blocks away, Postoffice Street—long ago a risqué red-light district, now respectably known as Gallery Row—offers art galleries, antiques stores, restaurants and pubs, and the magnificently restored Grand 1894 Opera House. The 1999–2000 season, for example, featured appearances by Tim Conway and Harvey Korman, Mandy Patinkin, Johnny Mathis, and the Australian dance group Tap Dogs; performances included *The Pirates of Penzance*, *Camelot*, *Showboat*, *Annie*, and many more.

PRACTICAL NOTES: A little advance planning will enhance your East End experience. Before the two of you leave for Galveston, make some phone calls and schedule your trip around the entertainment that interests you most. Contact the **Galveston Arts Center** (409–763–2403) to find out the **Art Walk** schedule. (Every six weeks or so, the art and antiques galleries along Postoffice Street throw open their doors for a Saturday-evening open house. It's great fun.) Call the **Grand 1894 Opera House** (409–765–1894 or 800–821–1894) for their schedule of performances. And finally, the **Old Quarter Acoustic Café** (409–762–9199) is Galveston's venue

Romance AT A GLANCE

♦ Snuggle with miniature bunnies at the charming **Victorian Inn** bed-and-breakfast (511 Seventeenth Street; 409–762–3235) in the heart of Galveston's historic East End.

♦ Listen to the pounding surf as you dine seaside on homemade pasta and fresh Gulf Coast seafood at **Mario's** (628 Seawall; 409–763–1693), a family-run island favorite.

♦ Borrow two of your inn's bicycles to roam the quiet streets of the historic East End. Around lunchtime, head for the deliciously hip **Mosquito Café** (628 Fourteenth Street; 409–763–1010). Spend your afternoon in the sun, combing the sandy shore for seashells.

♦ For dinner tonight, shall it be shellfish at the **Saltwater Grill** (2017 Postoffice Street; 409–762–3474) or sexy Latino cuisine at **Rudy & Paco's** (2028 Postoffice; 409–762–3696)? The delicious decision is all yours. Then choose a venue for sweet music together: either the magnificently restored **Grand 1894 Opera House** (2020 Postoffice; 409–765–1894) or the folksier, down-home environs of the **Old Quarter Acoustic Café** (413 Twentieth Street; 409–762–9199) should suit you to a T. Afterward, retreat to the snug **Old Cellar Bar** (2015 Postoffice; 409–763–4477) for a nightcap.

♦ Start your morning with a traditional Tex-Mex eye-opener, sharing spicy salsa and huevos at **The Original Mexican Café** (1401 Market; 409–762–6001). Then shop the art and antiques galleries on historic **Postoffice Street,** once the island's naughtiest avenue!

for live acoustic music, open year-round. This small, casual room is home to great folk music and a grown-up crowd of music lovers.

DAY ONE: evening

Your cozy home for the weekend is the beautifully restored **Victorian Inn** bed-and-breakfast (511 Seventeenth Street; 409–762–3235; $100 to $150), a red-brick Italianate villa built in 1899 and situated in the heart of Galveston's historic East End district.

All of the Victorian's antiques-furnished rooms are lovely, but the most romantic is the second-floor **Mauney's Suite** ($150 per night), with its king-size brass bed, private bath, and charming private veranda in the cupola. You'll have this little round porch to yourselves, overlooking a garden blooming with oleander, hibiscus, and gardenia. It's the perfect make-out spot, as well as a great vantage point for watching the antics of the miniature rabbits raised by innkeeper Marcy Hanson. (They race in dizzy circles around the lawn just below you.)

If the popular Victorian Inn is full on the weekend you want, try the quiet little **Away At Sea Inn** (1127 Church Street; 409–762–1668 or 800–762–1668; $125 to $145) instead. It's only a few blocks from the Victorian Inn and equally convenient for this itinerary. Of the three guest rooms in this snug Victorian cottage, we like the **Oriental Room** best ($145 per night) for its luxurious Jacuzzi built for two.

DINNER

After settling into your lodgings, you might enjoy a quiet cocktail on the veranda, delightfully alone at last or in the sociable company of your fellow guests. Toward sundown, drive across the island—only a dozen or so blocks wide at this point—to the Seawall. You can park just about anywhere and stroll along the wall's broad brim, a great vantage point for viewing the day's last rays over the waves. No doubt the sea breeze will stimulate your appetites, so as soon as you feel a hunger pang, saunter along to the corner of Seventh Street and Seawall to find your supper. Expect a warm welcome at **Mario's** (628 Seawall; 409–763–1693; moderate), which for twenty-five years has been as beloved by locals as it is by tourists. This family-owned-and-operated Italian restaurant offers a lusty list of perfectly prepared seafood pasta dishes like blackened shrimp fettuccine and mussels with linguini, but it is perhaps best known for veal, served grilled, Parmigiana, rollatini, Marsala, or Francese. Everyone at Mario's, from the hostess to the busboys, will make the pair of you feel like family, and the clean-lined modern dining room has a soothing view of the Seawall and the Gulf beyond.

DAY TWO: morning

BREAKFAST

Start your morning with breakfast at your lodgings. At the Victorian you'll find a buffet-style feast of freshly baked muffins, fruit dumplings, or quiche and, if it's your lucky day, Marcy Hanson's justly famous homemade banana bread. Join your fellow guests in the sunny, high-ceilinged dining room (Marcy says it's okay to come down in your bathrobe) or dine with your true love on your private, screened-in veranda.

Fortified by this glorious repast, you two will welcome a morning's spin. Borrow two of your inn's bicycles (both our listed accommodations provide complimentary bicycles for guests' use) for a **morning bicycle tour** of the East End's quiet, tree-lined streets. The historical district is bounded (roughly) by Broadway on the south and Market Street on the north, Nineteenth Street to the west, and Tenth Street to the east.

You can easily explore the quiet streets and avenues without fear of getting lost once you understand the street system, a simple grid of letters and numbers. The north-south cross streets are *numbered*, getting higher as you cycle west toward the Strand, lower if you ride east toward the Seawall and the Gulf. The east-west avenues are identified by *letters* as well as name; for example, Postoffice is also known as Avenue E, and Church is also known as Avenue F. The higher the letter in alphabetical order, the closer you are to Broadway.

Many of the most striking homes are on Sealy Avenue, but you will also find beautiful examples of Victorian architecture along Church, Ball, Winnie, and Postoffice Streets. Some highlights include the house at **1702 Ball Avenue** (corner of Ball and Seventeenth), gorgeously repainted and decorated with a sunflower motif. **1826 Sealy Avenue** is a double-galleried confection of gingerbread and latticework. Look for the matching two-story carriage house behind the stuccoed brick grandeur of **1728 Sealy Avenue.** The house at **1627 Sealy Avenue** is set at an eccentric diagonal on its lot, with a dramatically ramped entrance stair and mock tower.

Maybe neither of you can tell High Victorian from Romanesque Revival, or a town house from a cottage. That's okay; neither can we. But if you'd like to know more about the turn-of-the-twentieth-century architectural styles you see in the East End, there are several resources to tap. The **Strand Visitors Center** (2016 Strand; 409–765–7834) is a valuable source of historic information, maps, and brochures. The **East End Historical**

District Association (1501 Postoffice; 409–763–5928) publishes a handy guide called the *East End Historic District Riding and Walking Tour*. The ultimate compendium of island architecture is the ***Galveston Architectural Guidebook*** by Ellen Beasley and Stephen Fox, published by the Galveston Historical Foundation in 1996. This compact, portable volume is handsomely illustrated with photographs and maps and can be purchased at a number of Galveston's historical sites, including the Strand Visitors Center (above) and Midsummer Books (2311 Ship's Mechanic Row; 409–765–5930).

DAY TWO: afternoon

LUNCH

Around lunchtime plot your cycle course toward the **Mosquito Café** at the corner of Fourteenth and Winnie (628 Fourteenth Street; 409–763–1010; inexpensive). The Mosquito is a hip new addition to the East End, an airy, comfortable counter-service cafe with excellent quiches and frittatas, hearty sandwiches, homemade soups, and pastas. Check the chalkboard menus for such favorites as the Mambo roasted pork sandwich with house-made fruit chutney on fluffy, toasted focaccia bread, or the Asian noodle salad, made with angel hair pasta tossed with a colorful jumble of fresh lettuces, red cabbage, carrots, and bell peppers, dressed with sesame vinaigrette. Dine indoors under the ceiling fans or outdoors on the shady latticed patio. And check out the T-shirts sporting the cafe's clever logo; you might want to buy each other a souvenir.

Back at the Victorian after your tasty lunch, innkeeper Marcy swears she knows the best places on the island to find seashells. She'll draw you a map and even wash and pack the shells for you to take home. So grab your sunscreen and a bag for the treasures you'll find, like lightning whelks—the official seashell of Texas, mind you—and sand dollars. Tip: Check those shells for occupants before you bag 'em; you don't want to accidentally bring home a live hermit crab!

DAY TWO: evening

This evening you'll summon a horse-drawn carriage to chauffeur you in old-fashioned style to dinner; afterward, take in the live theater or musical performance of your choice in the heart of Postoffice Street's gallery district.

Ask your innkeeper to make arrangements for a horse-drawn carriage to ferry you and your beloved between your inn and Postoffice Street for the evening. The round-trip costs only $20 to $25 from the East End, more from locations farther away. To check pricing or book your own, call **Island Carriages** at (409) 765–6951 or **Seahorse Carriages** at (409) 925–3312.

DINNER

For dinner tonight, a fine kettle of fish awaits you at the **Saltwater Grill** (2017 Postoffice; 409–762–3474; moderate; reservations recommended), a sleek, sophisticated new addition to the island dining scene. Treat yourselves to lust-inspiring delicacies like cold-water Canadian oysters of the half-shell, juicy steamed mussels, or soulful seafood gumbo. You might perch together at the long, handsome bar to watch your shrimp scampi cook in those shiny steam-fired kettles, or settle back into high-backed booths better suited for whispering sweet nothings. Or join exuberant Nicaraguan host Francisco "Paco" Vargas at **Rudy & Paco's** (2028 Postoffice; 409–762–3696; moderate; reservations recommended), a sophisticated black-and-white room with the feel of a European bistro. The cosmopolitan menu has a sexy Latino accent, from the complimentary fried plantain chips with (addictive) chimichurri sauce for dipping to appetizers like *Vuelve a la Vida*—crab claws, calamari, and Gulf shrimp sautéed in white wine and garlic butter—which Paco swears is a proven aphrodisiac as well as a cure for hangovers! For dessert trade spoonfuls of the sweet, rich *Tres Leches*, a lacy white cake drenched with three kinds of cream.

Depending on your choice you'll spend the rest of the evening in the magnificently restored **Grand 1894 Opera House** (2020

Postoffice; 409–765–1894), just down the street from your dinner assignation, or in the folksier, down-home environs of the **Old Quarter Acoustic Café** around the corner (413 Twentieth Street, 409–762–9199). Either location is historic, just in different ways, you'll see.

The thousand-seat Grand 1894 Opera House was built in 1894, of course, at a cost of $100,000. Almost a century later its restoration to a glorious gem of rococo gilt and velvet was completed at a cost of nearly $8 million. At present, performances by the Joffrey Ballet, the Royal Shakespeare Theater Company of New York, the Dance Theatre of Harlem, Harry Belafonte, Bill Cosby, and Debbie Reynolds receive standing ovations from the same stage formerly graced by nineteenth-century stars like actress Sarah Bernhardt, ballerina Anna Pavlova, and conductor/composer John Philip Sousa.

The funky, friendly Old Quarter Acoustic Café has been a landmark on the Texas music circuit for years. The late Townes Van Zandt made many a memorable appearance on its stage, where now you can hear Texas legends like Shake Russell and Dana Cooper, the Sisters Morales, or Ray Wylie Hubbard. Then again, you might be treated to raucous sea chanties and drinking tunes from the crew of the *Elissa*—you just never know. Be sure you check out the characters seated with you in the audience, too; Dusty Hill of ZZ Top fame has been known to drop by.

After the show retreat to the snug, wood-paneled environs of the **Old Cellar Bar** (2015 Postoffice; 409–763–4477) for a nightcap. Sit side by side at its antique bar, which once graced the Paris Opera House. You'll find an excellent list of single-malt scotches and vintage brandies, wines by the glass, cigars, and cappuccinos.

DAY THREE: morning

BREAKFAST

Get off to a spicy start with a traditional Tex-Mex breakfast in another historical East End setting. **The Original Mexican Café** (1401 Market; 409–762–6001; inexpensive) claims to be the oldest continuously operating restaurant in Galveston. They scramble up some great eggs (ranchero, Mexicana, con chorizo, or papas) and breakfast burritos every weekend morning. It's a cheerful, home-style place, and you and your loved one will appreciate their thoughtful attention to heart-healthy guidelines.

After breakfast and checkout, spend the morning together admiring the art and antiques of Postoffice Street's **Gallery Row.** It's titillating to think that this oh-so-genteel neighborhood was at one time a naughty row of red-hot bordellos. Even better, Gallery Row is only a short stroll from the East End—but by all means take the car if you share a tendency to splurge on large purchases!

Some of our favorite stops include **Eiband's Gallery** (2201 Postoffice; 409–763–5495), which offers antique furnishings, jewelry, books, and rugs from a consortium of dealers, as well as oils and watercolors by the Galveston Art League and local artists. The **Leslie Gallery** (2208 Postoffice; 409–763–6370) is a framing studio that also offers original art as well as prints, including highly collectible Mardi Gras posters, past and present. The **Anderson-Kelver Studio** (2202 Postoffice; 409–763–2265) features the sights and seashores of Galveston rendered in watercolors and oils by two local artists.

Now loaded with treasures or trinkets, return to your car and settle in for the ride home to the mainland. You'll be glad of your souvenir remembrances as the island, and your magical weekend, recedes in the rearview mirror.

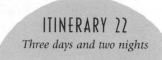

Seawall Promenade

ITHIN WALKING DISTANCE of the East End is Galveston's Seawall, a 7-mile-long monument to the determination of turn-of-the-century engineers, who built this wall and then literally raised the eastern end of the island 11 feet above sea level.

Since the Great Storm of 1900, the Seawall has protected Galveston from the ravages of hurricane-spawned storm surges and has provided a long, lovely promenade for its citizens. Now it's a seaside venue, lively beyond the wildest dreams of its nineteenth-century designers, thronged with joggers, bikers, tourists, and lovers, where beautiful bodies may been seen roller-blading and honey-mooners pedal sweet, surrey-fringed bicycles built for two.

DAY ONE: evening

Just a few short blocks from the Seawall is **The Coppersmith Inn** (1914 Avenue M; 409–763–7004 or 800–515–7444; $135 to $160), a beautifully restored and turreted Queen Anne home that gets its name from its previous Irish owner, who was—you guessed it!—a coppersmith.

While the Coppersmith's antique-furnished rooms in the main house are lovely, the very private accommodations separated from the main house by a brick patio and lush garden are ideal for your weekend tryst. The upstairs **Carriage House Suite** ($160 per night), with a vaulted timbered ceiling, has a whirlpool tub for two, while the bath of the bright and frilly **Clara's Country Cottage** ($135 per

*R*omance
AT A GLANCE

◆ Hide away this weekend in the delightfully private carriage house or honeymoon cottage at **The Coppersmith Inn** (1914 Avenue M; 409–763–7004 or 800–515–7444).

◆ Giggle at the vintage photos of flappers and bathing beauties at **Gaido's Seafood Restaurant** on the Seawall (3800 Seawall: 409–762–9625), where the strong suit has been Gulf Coast seafood for almost a century.

◆ Pedal a surrey or whiz along on roller blades on the broad sunny Seawall, checking out the buff bods and seabirds. Lunch is lazy and laid-back at **The Spot** (3204 Seawall; 409–621–5237). You've earned the sleek wedge of Key lime pie for dessert at the adjoining **Maddie's Bakery.**

◆ Ooh and aah at the towering glass pyramids of **Moody Gardens** (1 Hope Boulevard off Eighty-first Street; 409–744–7256 or 800–582–4673). Steal steamy kisses in the rain forest there . . . or don silly 3–D glasses for an **IMAX Theater** movie.

◆ Sip peach daquiris at sunset on the deck at **Fish Tales Seafood Grill** (Twenty-fifth and Seawall; 409–762–8545) and eat your fill of spicy boiled shrimp.

◆ Enjoy one last breakfast at your inn, then hop a trolley for a leisurely sight-seeing tour of historic Galveston.

night) boasts the very same antique tin tub seen in the Kenny Rogers movie *Gambler V*.

After you've made yourselves at home in the inn, take a predinner stroll through this lovely neighborhood. Many homes have been restored, and as many more are in that fascinating transitional phase between money pit and showplace. You'll feel your frazzled city nerves unwind as you slow to "island time" on these quiet streets.

DINNER

Tonight you'll enjoy dinner at **Gaido's Seafood Restaurant** on the Seawall (3800 Seawall; 409–762–9625; expensive), a Galveston favorite for more than eighty years. You can't miss the giant blue crab that tops the restaurant, but don't believe locals when they tell you it was caught in Galveston Bay! And don't miss Gaido's fascinating collection of historic Galveston photos,

especially the group shot of beauty contestants in "bathing costumes" circa 1924.

At Gaido's you can order your dinner "complete" or a la carte,
but be warned that complete dinners include an appetizer, a salad,
a full-sized entree *and* a rich dessert! Gaido's strong suit is seafood:
Gulf shrimp, Louisiana crawfish, bay oysters, and soft-shell crabs,
plus whatever's fresh for the catch of the day.

After dinner, drive back along the Seawall with your car windows
rolled down to luxuriate in the steady, soothing roar of the surf. You
may want to linger in the Coppersmith's fragrant garden by moonlight. Or turn in early to nestle together in your king-size bed. You'll
want a long, sound sleep before tomorrow's fun in the sun!

DAY TWO: morning

BREAKFAST

Breakfast is served as you like it at the Coppersmith. Lounge in bed
as late as you like; then dine al fresco on the shady brick patio or
join your fellow guests in the sunny, wood-paneled dining room.

Now don your sexiest exercise togs (and sunscreen) for a morning
bike ride along the broad surface of the Seawall. You can borrow
ordinary bicycles from your innkeepers, but why not **rent a pedal-
powered "surrey"** built for two, with a brightly striped and fringed
awning on top for shade? Surreys are available from many locations
along the Seawall (such as the Driftwood Motel, 3114 Seawall;
409–765–8579). Rental prices start at $10.00 per hour. The truly
ambitious may want to try roller blades instead, for only $7.00 per
hour.

As you whiz along the Seawall you can admire the buff bods,
deep tans, and colorful tattoos of the Seawall's show-off crowd, or
you can more modestly scope out the multitude of sea and shore
birds. Galveston is home to dozens of varieties of gulls, terns, sand-
pipers, egrets, herons, and pelicans; hundreds more species wing
through during the spring and fall migrations. Keep an eye out to
sea for bottle-nosed dolphins, too, frequently seen chasing mullet
and playing in the shallow surf.

DAY TWO: afternoon
LUNCH

Mardi Gras Madness

The Seawall is a people-watcher's paradise all year long, but for some certifiable craziness try it during the two-week-long Mardi Gras celebration. Weekend parades of floats, marching bands, and beauty queens snake along the Seawall and into the Strand District, with participants tossing beads, doubloons, and other goodies to crowds of roving revelers. The action is good-natured by day but naughty at night, when provocative costumes and outrageous behavior are de rigueur for normally staid island residents and their half-million party guests. There's something about peeking through a sexy sequined mask that will free your wildest urges . . .

Park your bike or blades long enough to hit **The Spot** (3204 Seawall; 409–621–5237; inexpensive) for lunch, a cheery, casual cafe where nobody will mind your healthy glow from exercising. The Spot is actually a collection of old wood-frame cottages moved lock, stock, and barrel from the town to the Seawall. Now gaily painted and dishing up made-to-order burgers and excellent onion rings, The Spot has air-conditioned seating indoors and a breezy deck facing the Seawall outdoors.

And you've certainly earned a hug and a treat for dessert. The Spot offers several flavors of Stucchi's ice cream, a locally popular brand, or check out **Maddie's Bakery** next door for pastries and home-style cookies. Their tart, creamy Key lime pie is outstanding; and you can pick up a loaf of fresh-baked bread to take home.

After all the pedaling and fresh air of the morning, you'll welcome the cool, soaring interiors of **Moody Gardens** (1 Hope Boulevard off Eighty-first Street; 409–744–7256 or 800–582–4673; Web site www.moodygardens.com), Galveston's newest entertainment attraction, situated on 242 acres of landscaped gardens. An improbable trio of glass pyramids glitters on the bay side of the island only a short drive from your inn. To get there drive west along Seawall, turn inland on Eighty-first Street, and then follow the signs.

Our fantasy favorites are the ten-story **Rainforest Pyramid,** with its lush tropical blooms, towering greenery, and shallow pool of exotic Amazon fish—a great setting for a steamy make-out session when nobody's looking; and the new **Aquarium Pyramid,** a shadowy underwater world teeming with shark, stingrays, and even penguins. (The Discovery Space Center Pyramid is too crammed with noisy children to be much fun for lovers.)

When you arrive, check to see what's playing at Moody Garden's **IMAX Theater,** with its six-story screen. The short-film subjects range from Mount Everest to the Serengeti, and some are three-dimensional, requiring you to wear bug-eyed (but not uncomfortable) goggles. If the two of you plan to see an IMAX feature film, buy your movie tickets first and then take a leisurely hand-in-hand stroll through the rain forest and aquarium before the film starts.

After the movie, you two can slip back to the room for a "power nap" or head on over to the Seawall in time for happy hour by the sea.

DAY TWO: evening

DINNER

This evening you'll dally and dine outdoors on the upper deck at **Fish Tales Seafood Grill** (Twenty-fifth and Seawall; 409–762–8545; moderate). From this lofty perch overlooking the Seawall you can toast each other and the sundown with frosty peach daiquiris. Start by swapping spicy Shrimp Kisses (bacon-wrapped shrimp stuffed with jalapeño peppers and cheese) or nibbling on the silky-smooth seared-tuna appetizer. Then move on to the three-way Shrimp Combo—fat jumbo shrimp fried, dipped in creamy Dijon sauce, or Cajun-seasoned and grilled. As the sky darkens over the rolling surf at your feet, seize the moment for a kiss or two. Afterward you might stay for live music in the bar downstairs or slip away for a moonlit stroll along the Seawall.

Back at your inn tonight might be the night for a long, luxurious soak in your whirlpool tub, to soothe those aching quads and stim-

ulate sexy thoughts. Light some candles first and chill a bottle of
bubbly in your room's refrigerator. Ahh, sheer bliss.

DAY THREE: morning

BREAKFAST

Sleep late and linger over breakfast at Coppersmith or, if you
can rouse yourselves, try the **Mosquito Café** (628 Fourteenth
Street, at the corner of Fourteenth and Winnie; 409–763–1010) for
frittatas, omelets, and some of the best fresh-baked breakfast pastries on the island. You'll particularly like their fresh blueberry
scones topped with lickable whipped cream . . . absolutely decadent.

Before you say goodbye to the island, allow a couple of hours
for a **scenic trolley ride** and tour of the Strand. Galveston's quaint
trolley system is a great way to sightsee, absolutely stress-free. Pick
up the trolley only a few blocks from your inn at 2100 Seawall; then
ride the rails over to 2016 Strand for only 60 cents. Once there, try
the Strand shopping guide from Itinerary 20 or check out the art galleries along nearby Postoffice Street listed in Itinerary 21.

Just Beachy

AST THE WESTERN END OF THE SEAWALL, the scenery gives way to mile after mile of blessedly underdeveloped beaches. Instead of hotels and condominiums, you'll find weathered wooden houses on tall stilts available for rental by the weekend or the week.

The firm sands of Galveston's beaches are a warm, tawny brown—perfect for building sandcastles—and home to dozens of varieties of shorebirds and seashells. Fishermen wade into the gentle surf, casting for flounder, speckled trout, or redfish; children splash in the shallows, and couples wander hand in hand along the tide line.

For lovers who want to get away from it all, to escape into a relaxed and easy world where dressing for dinner means putting on flip-flops and moonrise is the major event of the evening, Galveston's West End is heaven.

PRACTICAL NOTES: The best accommodations on the West End are the simple wood-frame houses that face the Gulf, perched on stilts just above the dunes and high-tide line. Most romantic are those right on the beach, of course, where the ocean fills your senses. Although many of these "front row" homes are large, designed for extended clans of families and friends, there are several smaller cottages, affordable and cozy, just right for a couple.

Of the smaller beachfront cottages available for weekend or weekly rental, we like **Watabeag** (21610 West Beach, in the Sea Isle subdivision; $425 per weekend), the **Beach House** (23170 West Beach in Terramar; $350 per weekend), and **Greenfloe** (13101 Bermuda Drive, in Bermuda Beach, $375 per weekend). These are

Romance AT A GLANCE

◆ Pick a romantic, fully furnished beach house for two from the cottages available for weekend or weekly rental through **Sand-N-Sea Properties** (409–737–2556 or 800–880–2554). Stock your shelves with delectable goodies from **Randall's Food Market** (2931 Central City Boulevard at Sixty-first Street; 409–744–0413) and local produce stands.

◆ Dine bayside at **Waterman** (14300 Stewart Road at Pirate's cove; 409–737–5824), where the water view from the back deck can't be beat.

◆ Gallop the beach on horseback, renting your pretty ponies from **Gulf Stream Stables** (8 Mile Road just off FM–3005; 409–744–1004). Couples that crave more power can find wave runners and jet skis available for rental on FM–3005 next to Beach Pocket Park #1.

◆ Lunch Texas home-style at **Jimmy Joe's Sports Café** (16708 San Luis Pass Road; 409–737–4665), then hit the beach to spend your afternoon in the sun. Go swimming or go fly a kite from the **Kites Unlimited** store (Seawall at Ninety-ninth Street; 409–744–4121).

◆ Get all the fixings for your own shrimp boil at **Allex's Seafood** (1727 Sixty-first Street; 409–741–1360), and then feast in barefoot glory on your beachhouse deck.

◆ Ride the **Bolivar Ferry** from the island to the mainland and back again, then brunch in Southern comfort at **Clary's** (8509 Teichman Road; 409–740–0771).

off-season prices, as many houses are only available by the week during the summer high season.

The friendly agents at **Sand-N-Sea Properties** (409–737–2556 or 800–880–2554) will help you choose the beach house just right for you. Preview rental property photos on their Web site at www.galveston.com/sandnsea/.

While all the rental houses are fully furnished, including kitchen gear and barbecue grills, you'll need to bring your own silk sheets, fluffy towels, and gourmet goodies. Don't forget to pack sunscreen!

If the two of you prefer posh to unpretentious, try **The Galvestonian** beachfront resort condos at the opposite end of the island (1401 East Beach Boulevard; 409–765–6161 or toll-free 888–

526–6161). This high-rise development is beautifully maintained, very private, and very much on the beach, with elevated swimming pool, hot tub, and tennis courts. All condos have fully equipped kitchens and fabulous Gulf views, but of the one-bedroom models, we prefer the larger Cortez floor plan for its two balconies: one from the living room and an additional one off the bedroom. It's those little things that make the difference! Nightly rates range from $125 off-season weekday to $255 on-season weekend; weekly rates $665 off-season to $915 on-season.

DAY ONE: evening

On the way to your beach house, stop by the Randall's grocery store on Sixty-first Street for the best selection of good beach food: Croissants, coffee, and fresh fruit make great starters. Then, as you drive west along Seawall Boulevard (which becomes FM–3005 past the western end of the Seawall), look for a farmer selling fresh produce from the back of his pickup truck, parked just before the flashing traffic light at 8 Mile Road. Neighbors call him "Tomato Man" for the luscious ripe Tennessee tomatoes he sells, and often he has delightful herb-flower honey, too.

DINNER

After settling into your beach house for the weekend, reward your-selves with a fresh seafood dinner at **Waterman** (14300 Stewart Road, at Pirate's Cove; 409–737–5824; moderate). This spacious restaurant has the woodsy feel of a luxury lodge, with a thick oriental carpet on the stair landing and a high beamed ceiling. The west-facing back wall is all window, leading onto a spacious outdoor deck and a sweeping view of Galveston Bay. On breezy evenings the deck and the view can't be beat.

Try Gulf Coast standards like the jumbo fried shrimp, crisp and peppery, or smoky, dark seafood gumbo loaded with shrimp and oysters. Or indulge yourself with more exotic fare, like a beautifully grilled fillet of Idaho trout topped with red and black caviar and lightly drizzled with lemon butter. For dessert treat yourselves to the fresh berries dripping with rich saboyan, a foamy custard sauce whipped with wine.

Back at the beach, kick off your shoes and stroll along the firm sand by the light of the moon. This is the time, and the place, for a passionate embrace.

DAY TWO: morning

BREAKFAST

Slip into something comfortable and make your own breakfast from the fruit and honey and croissants you had the forethought to pick up last night. Dine barefoot in the sunshine on your own deck. Sit back, smell the coffee, listen to the laughing gulls. A salt-air kiss or two may lead to something better . . .

After lunch it's time for some serious rest and relaxation on the beach. Consult our list of beaches for one that suits your fancy or lounge on the sand right in front of your house. Collect shells, float in the warm shallow water, or read romantic novels aloud under the shade of your beach umbrellas.

Another restful alternative: Take a nap. Don't laugh! Whether entwined in a double hammock hung from a shady corner of your deck or sprawled across a king-size bed under a lazily twirling ceiling fan, naps can be one of your vacation's little shared luxuries.

Or go fly a kite! You can't miss the **Kites Unlimited** store (Seawall at Ninety-ninth Street; 409–744–4121); just look for a flotilla of brightly colored kites flying in the breeze above this store at the western end of the Seawall. Here you two will find everything you need for an afternoon of young-at-heart fun: the diamond-shaped kites of your childhood, soaring bilevel parafoils, and tricky two-handed stunt kites, plus rollers of string, and even glowing cyalume light sticks for nighttime flights.

Did you hear that truck drive through your subdivision this morning, bell clanging? No, that wasn't the ice-cream man; it was the shrimp man. Some of the freshest catch in Galveston can be had from these local entrepreneurs who prowl the West End neighborhoods every weekend morning.

Throw on a pair of blue jeans and boots and head out for a morning horseback gallop along the beach. What could possibly be more romantic? Gulf Stream Stables (8 Mile Road, just off FM–3005; 409–744–1004), which offers well-kept horses for rental by the hour, opens daily at 9:30 A.M., year-round. Tack is Western, and dress is decidedly casual—don't worry that you left your hunting pinks at home.

Perhaps you and your sweetie are more the daredevil, skimpy-bathing-suit types. For thrills, chills, and most definitely spills, how about an invigorating spin on a jet ski? Wave runners and jet skis are available for rental next to Beach Pocket Park #1, just a mile past the west end of the Seawall before 8 Mile Road. They offer lessons for beginners and tours for more experienced skiers at $35 per half hour. They're open from 10:00 A.M. to sundown daily.

DAY TWO: afternoon

LUNCH

After this morning's outdoorsy workout, the two of you should have worked up a healthy appetite for a home-style lunch. Forget about counting fat grams and drive straight to **Jimmy Joe's Sports Café** (16708 San Luis Pass Road; 409–737–4665) in Jamaica Beach. Join the fishermen and golfers for Texas favorites like a chicken-fried steak sandwich with cream gravy and French fries, or chili pie—a steaming bowl of spicy meat chili ladled over Fritos corn chips.

DAY TWO: evening

DINNER

Be on the lookout for the shrimp truck in preparation for fixing tonight's intimate dinner for two at your beach house. If you missed the shrimp man this morning, John Allex at **Allex's Seafood & Bait** (1727 Sixty-first Street; 409–741–1360) will set you up not only with the shrimp but also cooking tips, should you need them. Buy some jumbo shrimp and a packet of "shrimp boil" seasoning, steam some ears of corn and new potatoes, chill a bottle of white wine, and feast barefoot on your deck by candlelight. Dessert? Brownies and ice cream, of course. The beach's pleasures are simple and elemental.

Guide to Galveston's Beaches

All 32 miles of Galveston's beaches are open public access. You can park in designated areas and go wherever you like. If you're not actually staying on the beach, though, you might like amenities—rest rooms, showers, concession stands, or umbrella rentals—so check out these state and county beach "parks."

Stewart Beach (Seawall Boulevard at Broadway; 409–765–5023) is the best known and liveliest—or crowded, depending on your point of view—of all Galveston's beaches. Volleyball tournaments, sand-castle competitions, and concerts are regularly scheduled throughout summer, plus a miniature golf course and bumper boats. Amenities include umbrella and beach-chair rentals, pavilion with snack bar, souvenir shop, rest rooms, and showers.

East Beach/Apffel Park (Seawall and Boddeker Drive; 409–762–3278). All the way at the eastern end of the island, East Beach is also lively since it's one of the few Galveston beaches on which consumption of alcoholic beverages is allowed, but it's rarely as crowded as Stewart. The annual AIA Sandcastle Competition is held here, and live music concerts are frequently scheduled. Great bird-watching at the Big Reef Nature Park. Amenities include pavilion with snacks and outdoor bar, picnic areas, gift shop, rest rooms, and showers. (Open mid-March through mid-October; parking fee $5.00.)

Galveston Island State Park (FM–3005, West of 13 Mile Road; 409–737–1222). Holiday weekends can get crowded here, as many families camp out, taking advantage of the electrical hookups; otherwise, there's plenty of elbow room. Other amenities include picnic tables and barbecue pits. The park is open daily year-round; admission is $3.00 per person.

Galveston County Beach Pocket Parks (Two locations on FM–3005; 409–770–5358). Perfect for a summer day trip, Pocket Park #3 offers rest rooms, snack bar, and umbrella and beach-chair rentals. Pocket Park #2 was damaged by tropical storm Frances in 1998, so as of this writing, it has only portable toilets; renovation, though, is underway. (Pocket Park #1 has been permanently closed, in case you were wondering.) Both Pocket Parks are open from Memorial weekend until roughly the end of September. Parking fee is $5.00 per vehicle.

After dinner take a long walk together along the beach. You'll have the sand, the surf, the moon, and the stars all to yourself on any given stretch of West Beach at night, with nobody to catch you kissing. This end of the island is so quiet and dark that you'll be able to see constellations all the way down to the horizon, and even the lights of offshore oil platforms and shrimp boats twinkle festively over the Gulf.

DAY THREE: morning

Load up the car and eat a light breakfast; then spend your last morning on a **ferry ride** out on the waves—followed by a decadent Sunday brunch, of course.

Drive east along the Seawall until just past Broadway; then turn left on Ferry Road and follow the signs for the **Bolivar Ferry.** The short round-trip ride from the island to the mainland and back again is fun, and it's free. Compliments of the State of Texas, ferries continuously shuttle cars and pedestrians between the easternmost tip of Galveston Island to the Bolivar Peninsula. It's about a fifteen-minute minicruise each way.

Once your car is stowed safely aboard, you can climb to the observation deck to admire the panoramic views of Galveston Harbor, Pelican Island, and the Gulf of Mexico. Look for the blackened tower of the now-retired Bolivar Lighthouse, at present privately owned and not open to the public, alas. Take a bag of bread scraps to feed the seagulls from the rear of the ferry and take turns spotting the bottle-nosed dolphins that play in the channel.

On the peninsula you might want to see the small fleet of commercial shrimp boats at Point Bolivar (drive off the ferry and turn inland on Loop 108 and head through the town until 108 dead-ends); or check out the Bolivar Beach "Flats" (from the ferry landing turn right on Loop 108, toward the Gulf of Mexico). This wide, flat expanse of beach has shallow, smooth surf and is great for shelling or bird-watching. Otherwise, hop right back on the ferry for the return trip to the island, where brunch awaits you.

DAY THREE: afternoon

BRUNCH

Spend your Sunday afternoon as savvy islanders do: Drive out to **Clary's** (8509 Teichman Road; 409–740–0771; expensive; reservations recommended) around noontime for a relaxed Sunday brunch. (From the ferry landing head back toward Broadway and turn inland. Just before the causeway, exit Teichman Road and turn left.)

In a long, low bungalow tucked away on an inlet of Offats Bayou, across the shallows of Galveston Bay from the pyramids of Moody Gardens, affable owner Clary Milburn has been pampering celebrities and locals alike with Southern-style seafood for more than twenty years. (In the 1996 film *The Evening Star*, Jack Nicholson and Shirley MacLaine dine at Clary's.)

Sundays at Clary's feature a classical guitarist and eye-opening Bloody Marys. The rattan chairs are thickly cushioned, the bar well stocked, the tables draped with linen, and the waiters fitted out with tuxedos. (Although laid-back, this is definitely *not* a T-shirt and shorts place.) Indulge yourselves with the unabashedly retro Special Butter Lump Crab dish, chunks of fresh blue crab dowsed with melted butter, studded with green onions and bacon bits, then covered with a thick blanket of bright gold Cheddar cheese and run under the broiler to melt. When you can't make up your mind, the Saralyn B. platter—a smaller ramekin of the infamous butter crab, flanked by reasonable portions of grilled oysters and baked shrimp—is great but expensive, at $21.50. Fiddle-dee-dee, Miss Scarlett, you can worry about that tomorrow . . . at Tara.

Out in the Country

ℬrenham

BLUEBONNETS AND BLUE BELL

LTHOUGH THE COUNTRY TOWN of Brenham is only an hour and a half's drive northwest of Houston on one of the state's premiere "bluebonnet byways," it seems a whole world away from the big city. A picturesque haven for antiques and rose gardens, Brenham is also home to the Blue Bell Creameries, churning out what is modestly described as the best ice cream in the country. You and your sweetheart will revel in the slower, small-town pace of life here, where each passerby greets you with a cheery "Good morning!" and really means it.

PRACTICAL NOTES: The green hills of Brenham turn blue as the sky during **bluebonnet season** each spring. The painterly wildflower displays usually run from March to May, reaching a breathtaking crescendo in April. The first weekend in May brings the annual **Maifest,** a German-heritage festival celebrated round these parts since 1884, featuring all the bratwurst and sauerkraut you can eat, plenty of beer to wash it down with, and cheerful oom-pah serenades from assorted polka bands. Then in September the **Washington County Fair** comes to town, complete with rodeo riding, a livestock show, and a carnival. (For more events and information, check the Chamber of Commerce Web site at www.brenhamtx.org.)

DAY ONE: afternoon

Try to break away from Houston early today to catch one of the week-days-only tours of the **Blue Bell Creameries** (1101 South Horton

Romance AT A GLANCE

◆ Begin your country weekend by sampling sweet frozen treats at the **Blue Bell Creameries** (1101 South Horton Street; 979–836–7977 or 800–327–8135).

◆ Settle into a multiwindowed corner room of the historic **Ant Street Inn** (107 West Commerce; 979–836–7393; www.antstreetinn.com) in downtown Brenham.

◆ Chow down on monstrous chicken-fried steaks swimming in cream gravy at the **Country Inn II** (1000 East Horton Street; 979–836–2396).

◆ Tour historic downtown Brenham's quaint gift and antiques shops, starting with the **Brenham Heritage Museum** (105 South Market Street; 979–830–8445). Eat lunch soda-parlor-style at **Must Be Heaven** (107 West Alamo; 979–830–8536), then take a drive in the country to see the darling miniature horses raised by nuns at the **Monastery of St. Clare** (9300 Highway 105; 979–836–9652).

◆ Dine at an authentic 1950s-era **Sonic Drive-In** (1600 South Market Street; 979–836–4242). Shoot some pool at a local billiards parlor or choose companionable porch rockers for stargazing.

◆ Take a road less traveled back to Houston and stop by the **Pleasant Hill Winery** (1441 Salem Road; 979–830–VINE) for a tour and a taste.

Street; 979–836–7977 or 800–327–8135). Take US–290 west from Houston; then turn right on FM–577, which becomes Horton Street. (Note that "FM" stands for "farm to market" road.) The well-marked creamery entrance is 2 miles down the road on the right.

The forty-minute guided tours demonstrate how "the best ice cream in the country" is made, starting with a tongue-in-cheek video and ending with a tongue-in-scoop sampling of popular Blue Bell flavors. (Tour times are usually set for 10:00 and 11:00 A.M., 1:00, 1:30, 2:00, and 2:30 P.M., but do call ahead to confirm.) When you've licked your ice-cream cups clean, you can step into Blue Bell's **Country Store** to browse a charming collection of spotted-cow souvenirs.

DAY ONE: evening

Your home this weekend is the beautifully restored **Ant Street Inn** (107 West Commerce; 979–836–7393; $85 to $165; www.antstreetinn.com) in downtown Brenham. From the Blue Bell gates, turn right (north) on Horton Street to its intersection with Main Street. Turn left on Main (it's one-way the right way) and follow it into downtown Brenham. Turn left on Park Street and proceed to Commerce Street to find your inn.

Unlike so many bed-and-breakfasts that were once private homes, the Ant Street Inn began its life as a turn-of-the-century commercial building. As a result, the ceilings are higher and the rooms are much larger than you'd otherwise expect. Innkeepers Pam and Tommy Traylor have lovingly furnished the place with period antiques, but they've not forgotten the modern amenities, either, like private baths, cable television, and modem data ports in every room. (As if you'd even dream of bringing your laptop computer on this romantic getaway, right?)

Each of the fourteen guest rooms boasts exposed brick walls and stained glass, but our favorite for romance is the Galveston Room ($165 per night), a northeast corner room flooded with light from two walls of tall arched windows. The queen-size bed is dramatically carved and canopied, and a tub for two stands at the ready. As of this writing, the Traylors were hard at work on a new guest room that just might steal your heart when finished: The first-floor San Antonio Room ($235 per night) will have a decadently couple-sized tub, too, but also a brick fireplace and handsome Spanish beamed ceiling.

Check into your room and take your time to unpack and unwind. Freshen up, test the tub taps, bounce on the bed. If this playfulness leads to something more promising, then follow your hearts.

DINNER

Dress casually for dinner tonight—remember, you're in the country now, so jeans and boots are de rigueur. On your way out stop by Ant Street's paneled wine bar on the first floor for a cool glass of wine or beer and a friendly chat with your fellow guests. Many are Ant Street regulars and can offer advice on area activities and sightseeing.

Then hop in the car for the short drive to the **Country Inn II** (1000 East Horton Street; 979–836–2396; moderate), just the other side of downtown. Head north on Park Street and then turn right on Horton; you'll shortly see the restaurant on the right.

The unpretentious Country Inn specializes in steaks, steaks, and more steaks, cooked however you like but most often chicken-fried in jackets of crisp browned batter awash in peppery cream gravy. These fresh cut slabs-o-meat *start* at a pound, mind you, and range up to three and a half pounds, so bring your appetite. Look around you to the John Wayne memorabilia on the walls for heroic inspiration.

After dinner toddle back to Ant Street fat and happy. There's not much to do in downtown Brenham after dark, so plan to make your own entertainment. The game table in the corner of the Galveston Room's sitting area would be just right for a genteel game of Hearts or even a hand or two of strip poker, you wicked things.

DAY TWO: morning

BREAKFAST

Breakfast is served in the downstairs dining room that doubled as a wine bar last night, or, if you make arrangements in advance, it can be luxuriously served on a tray to your room.

This morning you'll take a leisurely walking tour of historic downtown Brenham, the area centered on the Washington County courthouse. This quaint portion of town was laid out in 1844, back when Texas was still a republic, and it still has that unmistakable feel of long ago.

We suggest you start at the **Brenham Heritage Museum** (105 South Market Street; 979–830–8445) to orient yourselves to the rich history of the area. From your inn walk north on Park Street to Alamo Street and turn right. At Market Street turn left, and you'll see the imposing brick facade of the museum on the right. The building, which used to be the town's post office, now houses an interesting permanent collection ranging from Indian artifacts to an antique steam-powered fire engine; don't miss the photo album documenting the history of Blue Bell ice cream.

Stroll back along Main Street and turn left on Baylor to find the **Country Co-op Antique Mall** (107 South Baylor; 979–830–0679), two stories jammed with quilts, china, and other collectibles. (On our last visit Confederate officers' swords were on sale at a 20 percent discount.) There's a counter here selling—you guessed it!—hand-scooped Blue Bell ice cream.

Return to Main Street and continue west to the corner of Douglas and Main to find **Glissman's** (106 West Main; 979–830–9100). This former drugstore turned souvenir shop still sports its original soda fountain, where you can get a delicious old-fashioned malted or . . . enjoy some Blue Bell ice cream.

Now walk south along Douglas Street back onto Alamo and explore the gift and antiques shops on the north side of the street, including **Linda and Company** (120 West Alamo; 979–836–3928) and **Nellie's Boutique and Gallery** (200 West Alamo; 979–830–1756).

DAY TWO: afternoon

LUNCH

Your walking tour has conveniently landed you right across the street from **Must Be Heaven** (107 West Alamo; 979–830–8536; inexpensive), a lovely lunch spot marked with a you-can't-miss-it spotted-cow sign. Inside, Must Be Heaven has captured the nostalgic atmosphere of an old-time soda parlor, complete with brass soda pulls and a pair of ornate jukeboxes. Choose from a dozen different sandwiches—we like the grilled chicken breast or the New Orleans–inspired muffaletta—plus a variety of soups, salads, and quiches. Do leave room for dessert, as the homemade cookies, pies, and cakes are irresistible. Or, you might succumb to some more of that Blue Bell ice cream . . .

After lunch you can take your car to explore farther afield. Drive south on Market Street out of downtown; then turn left (east) on Stone Street for a scenic route lined with pretty country homes. Turn left when you reach Horton Street to start your afternoon adventures at **Ellison's Greenhouses** (visitor entrance at 1808 South Horton Street; 979–836–6011), an impressive five-acre spread of hothouse blossoms and foliage plants. Depending on the season you might find thousands of fiery poinsettias or ranks of waxy, white Easter lilies. Call ahead if you'd like to tour the greenhouses; otherwise, content yourselves with the collection of trailing ivies, winter bulbs, and more at the gift shop (whose fragrant alcoves offer plenty of privacy for a quick, sweet kiss).

Those Painted Ladies
of the Prairies

It was presumably the women settlers of Texas who sentimentally christened Lupinus texensis (Fabaceae) the "bluebonnet," as the shape of
the hooded sapphire blossoms reminded them of the sunbonnets they
wore to protect their complexions from the fierce summer sun. As histo-
rian Jack Maguire later rhapsodized, "The bluebonnet is to Texas what
the shamrock is to Ireland, the cherry blossom to Japan, the lily to
France, the rose to England and the tulip to Holland." You don't need
to know that there are five different varieties of the Texas state flower to
appreciate them as Texans do. Just wade out into an ocean of azure
blossoms, plop yourself down, and pose for sappy photographs. Lovers,
spouses, children, pets, and even prize cattle are memorialized in keepsake albums across the state.

Keep an eye on your wristwatches to time your arrival at the
Monastery of St. Clare (9300 Highway 105; 979–836–9652) between
2:00 and 4:00 P.M., when the grounds are open to lay visitors. It's about
a fifteen-minute drive, 9 miles east of town. Travel north on Horton
Street and then turn right (northeast) on Highway 105; look for the
monastery on the right just past the FM–2193 turnoff.

Here the Franciscan Poor Clare nuns raise adorable miniature
horses, which you're welcome to pet—you won't be able to resist,
we predict—and photograph. You two can stroll around the peaceful, quiet grounds hand in hand and browse the Art Barn gift shop
for the nuns' handmade ceramics. For a moment of spiritual respite
and renewal, take a pew in the chapel and quietly contemplate your
good fortune in love.

DAY TWO: evening

DINNER

Dinner tonight will be a trip down memory lane for those
old enough to remember drive-in dining and a delightful
surprise for those too young to have ever been served by a carhop.
A few blocks south of downtown, on Market Street just past Tom

Green, you'll find the authentic 1950s-era **Sonic Drive-In** (1600 South Market Street; 979–836–4242; inexpensive), still bustling after all these years. Tune your car radio to the local oldies station; then order classic burgers and fries or chili dogs and onion rings through the intercom. After dark—the Sonic's open till 10:00 P.M. every night—you can steam up your windshield with some heavy petting to the strains of "Teen Angel" or "Under the Boardwalk."

Back in town, if you're looking for a little action, stop by **Legends Billiards** (100 West Main Street; 979–251–7665) on the courthouse square. You can impress each other with your pool-shooting prowess or watch a game on the bar's large-screen television. Place a little love wager to make things interesting. Otherwise, settle into side-by-side rocking chairs on the Ant Street Inn's rear balcony, overlooking the quiet courtyard. Tip your heads back to take in the night sky, afire with more stars than you'll ever see back in Houston.

DAY THREE: morning

BREAKFAST

Enjoy your good-bye breakfast at Ant Street or stroll down Alamo Street to the **Fluff Top Roll** restaurant (210 East Alamo; 979–836–9441; inexpensive) for a hearty, country-style breakfast served from 8:00 to 11:00 A.M. on Sundays. Toss cholesterol caution to the wind and indulge your appetites for those elemental things like sausage and biscuits and gravy or nibble the airy yeast rolls that lend this simple cafe its name.

Now load up the car for the return trip to Houston. Instead of retracing your steps on US–290, you can take Highway 36 south from Brenham through Bellville to Sealy, where you can pick up Interstate 10 east back into the big city. This scenic return route adds a mere 10 miles to your trip, and variety, after all, is the spice of both life and love.

FOR MORE ROMANCE

Before leaving Brenham behind turn right (west) on Salem Road from Highway 36—just past the sprawling Wal-Mart center on the left—to find the **Pleasant Hill Winery** (1441 Salem Road; 979–830–VINE). Free tours begin and end in the vineyard's hilltop barn, where you'll find a whimsical corkscrew collection displayed among other winemaking artifacts. But who are we kidding? The highlight of this expedition is in the tasting room, where you can sample the fruits of the vine. More wines and other, nonfermented souvenirs are for sale in the gift shop. (Note: This stop is especially festive during harvest weekends in July and August.)

Brenham and Burton
KING COTTON AND OLD ROSES

O YOU TWO *REALLY* WANT TO get away from it all? The countryside around Brenham is so quiet it makes even this burg's sleepy center seem like a busy metropolis. This short-but-sweet itinerary puts you out to pasture, so to speak, at a pretty working ranch northwest of town. There's a real possibility you won't want to do any of the activities that we've listed here, but we won't mind and neither will you: This weekend is all about getting in touch with yourselves and each other. Just sit on the porch or lounge in a hammock. Pet the dogs. Doze, dream, make love. Enjoy.

PRACTICAL NOTES: Since you'll be so far from civilization—or, you'll feel that way, at least—you may want to bring some frolicsome accoutrements with you. May we suggest a picnic blanket, a bottle of champagne, and perhaps some massage oil or bubble bath? While you're at it, toss in a well-chosen volume of romantic poetry and a heart-throb movie on video.

A very special time to visit the Antique Rose Emporium, a mecca for bloom enthusiasts, is the first weekend of November, when its fall festival draws hundreds of floral fanatics from all over the country. Call (979) 836–5548 for more information.

DAY ONE: morning

Get an early start from Houston to hit Brenham by mid-morning; then spend some time lazily kicking around downtown Brenham. Use the agenda suggested in the previous itinerary or try exploring

Romance
AT A GLANCE

◆ Stroll and shop your way across downtown Brenham; then pick up a picnic lunch at **Must Be Heaven** (107 West Alamo; 979–830–8536). Drive out of town to the incredibly romantic grounds of the **Antique Rose Emporium** (9300 Lueckemeyer Road; 979–836–5548) to feast al fresco on the velvety grass.

◆ Love will flourish in the middle of nowhere, way out at the **Mariposa Ranch Bed and Breakfast** (8904 Mariposa Lane, off FM–390; 979–836–4737); dinner is country-chic French at André Delacroix's **Brazos Belle** in nearby Burton (600 North Main Street, Burton; 979–289–2677).

◆ Exploring the **Burton Farmers Cotton Gin and Museum** (Burton; 979–289–3378) will give you a new feeling for Places in the Heart. Follow with a hearty blue-plate lunch at the homestyle **Burton Café** (12513 West Washington Street, Burton; 979–289–3849).

◆ On the way home check out the real-Texas cutting-horse action at the **Nueces Canyon Equestrian Center** (8 miles west of Brenham on US–290; 979–289–5600 or 800–925–5058).

this different route, lined with equally intriguing shops.

Park anywhere in Brenham. Then, working your way west to east on Alamo Street, start at the country-quaint **Brenham General Store** (207 West Alamo Street; 979–836–7231); then drop in on the doll's tea party at **Lil Angels Doll Shoppe** (just off Alamo at 116 South Park Street; 979–277–0913). Consider the possibilities of the intriguingly demure nighties and seductive aromatherapy fragrances at **Four Friends** (214 East Alamo; 979–836–3566). If you forgot to pack your scented candles, this is the place to pick some up. Then cross up to Main Street to adorn your beloved in shining silver at **Peter Emerson Silversmith** (205 East Main Street; 979–251–7747).

DAY ONE: afternoon

LUNCH

 End your downtown shopping spree at **Must Be Heaven** (107 West Alamo; 979–830–8536; inexpensive), where you'll pick out the makings of a picnic lunch. Eminently packable goodies include flaky-crusted quiches, thick sandwiches spread with buttery avocado and bean sprouts, or tried-and-true PB&J, along with chilled cups of fresh fruit and homemade chocolate chip cookies for dessert.

Then you'll drive out to the **Antique Rose Emporium** (9300 Lueckemeyer Road; 979–836–5548) for a splendid picnic on the grass. From downtown head east on one-way Alamo Street; then turn left (north) on Chappell Hill, which leads you to Highway 105. From 105 veer left on FM–50 and follow it about 15 miles north to the tiny community of Independence. You'll see the rolling acres of the Emporium on the right.

Even when the romantic old roses aren't in bloom, the Rose Emporium's eight-acre grounds are gorgeous, the landscaped green hills dotted with native plantings, ponds, fountains, and picturesque restored buildings. Take your time touring the fragrant gardens and those old cabins: The dim interior of the 1850s-era saltbox house is just right for a very private, very passionate embrace. Above the gardens is a thickly grassed slope where you two can spread a blanket or, if the ground's damp, choose a picnic table for your love feast. Whip out that paperback edition of Shakespeare's sonnets you had the forethought to pack and read dreamily aloud to your beloved.

Rosarians and Rustlers

Michael Shoup, owner of the Antique Rose Emporium, describes himself alternately as a "rosarian" and a "rose rustler," a lover of wild roses dedicated to saving the thorny beauties wherever they may grow. A rose, like love, can flourish in the least likely places: One of his found blossoms, rescued from a Houston roadside, is christened "Highway 290 Pink Buttons." Shoup ultimately built his business around the blooms he admires so much for their fragrance, diversity, and strength. If your love is like a red, red rose, it would seem you're in luck; long after their homesteads crumbled, these gorgeous flowers survived.

Around mid-afternoon you'll be ready to check into your accommodations at the **Mariposa Ranch Bed and Breakfast** (8904 Mariposa Lane off FM–390; 979–836–4737; www.mariposaranch.com; $80 to $250 per night). To get there from the Rose Emporium, you'll travel west on the delightfully scenic La Bahia Highway, also known more prosaically as FM–390. You'll find the Ranch turnoff ½ mile before you reach Highway 36 North.

There are two beautiful rooms in the main house at Mariposa, as well as pretty little cabins scattered across the grounds. Honeymooners often choose the shady Fern Oaks Cottage, and we love the rustic authenticity of the Texas Ranger's 1825 log cabin, with its huge stone fireplace and steep steps to the sleeping loft. But on a recent visit we realized that the often-overlooked Bunkhouse, out by the ranch's real barn, is your best bet for togetherness. No cowboy would recognize this snug two-room cabin as a rough bunkhouse, thanks to its queen-size bed, sitting room with full kitchen, and a luxurious whirlpool for two in the large bathroom. There's a gas-log fireplace in the bedroom that'll warm things up in a hurry and a full-size refrigerator to chill your bubbly. Really, what more could you ask for romance?

DAY ONE: evening

DINNER

You've a special treat in store this evening at the **Brazos Belle** in nearby Burton (600 North Main Street, Burton; 979–289–2677 or 713–868–9466; moderate to expensive), a chic French restaurant cleverly disguised in the restored shell of an 1870s-era general store. From the ranch turn right on FM–390 West and follow it across Highway 36 North for about 10 miles; the Brazos Belle is on the left just past Burton's sole gas station and convenience store. This drive is particularly scenic at sunset, you'll find.

Chef/owner André Delacroix escaped from Houston's Four Seasons hotel and retired to the country, where he dishes out Provençal favorites and homemade bread on weekends only. (That honey-crusted wheat bread is so good you may want to inquire about purchasing a loaf to take home with you.) We're especially fond of his pâté, for starters, followed by his signature salmon fillet,

scented with lemongrass, or the meltingly tender grilled beef tenderloin. If the evening's fine, you two might want to take your post-
prandial coffee out on the wide front veranda, where you can watch
very few cars go by. Word to the wise: Bring plenty of cash or a personal check, as the Brazos Belle doesn't accept credit cards, and
nothing puts a crimp in your style like being mortally embarrassed
when the tab arrives.

Now slowly ease on back to the ranch. After dark it can be difficult
to spot the ranch entrance—and it really gets dark out here in the
country; just look at those stars!—so remember that it's only ½ mile
past Highway 36; if you go farther, you've missed it. Aren't you glad
now that you had the foresight to chill that champagne? Pop the
cork and toast each other with sips and kisses while the enormous
whirlpool tub slowly fills. Toss a handful of bath salts in the tub,
maybe, light a scented candle, and soak your cares away.

DAY TWO: morning

Chances are you'll wake with the sun, long before the ranch's designated 9:00 A.M. breakfast time. Snuggle into the twin terry-cloth
robes thoughtfully provided by your hosts and start the coffeemaker
in your cabin. Take your steaming mugs out to the porch, where no
doubt the ranch dogs will be thrilled to see you. Go ahead and pet
them while you enjoy the dawn; they're friendly and wiggling and
irresistible.

BREAKFAST

By breakfast time you'll be famished, so shower (together) and put on
your ranch duds; then stroll up to the main house, where breakfast is
served in the dining room, family style. It's a great opportunity to chat
with your fellow guests while you dig into broiled ruby red grapefruit,
scrambled eggs, and French toast or fresh blueberry muffins.

After breakfast wander through the Mariposa grounds a bit with
your camera to take some souvenir snapshots and say a lingering

good-bye. You two can hang out in the shady double hammock over by the Texas Ranger's cabin or lounge in rocking chairs on the front porch of the main house.

Feeling energetic? You can set off on a mini-expedition to see a gen-u-wine cotton gin back in Burton, restored under the aegis of the Smithsonian Institution. Remember the state of Sally Field's poor cotton-picking hands in the film *Places in the Heart*? Well, the **Burton Farmers Cotton Gin and Museum** (Burton; 979–289–3378) can give you some appreciation for the harshness of life when cotton was king. The museum is open on Friday and Saturday from 10:00 A.M. to 4:00 P.M., with $3.00 tours scheduled at 11:00 A.M. and 1:30 and 3:30 P.M. Additional tours are scheduled on request; just call ahead to make an appointment.

DAY TWO: afternoon

LUNCH

After your cotton-gin tour, where better to stop for lunch than the home-style **Burton Café** (12513 West Washington Street, Burton; 979–289–3849; inexpensive), to dine in the company of local farmers and ranchers? You'll find hearty blue-plate specials of roast beef or fried chicken, and mashed potatoes—with plenty of gravy—every day except Sunday. Don't overlook the homemade pies, either.

If it's Sunday, then we recommend a detour over to nearby Round Top for lunch at **Royers' Round Top Café** (979–249–3611), as described in the next itinerary. From Burton follow the signs for US–290 West toward Austin; then take the Round Top exit on Highway 237; it's only a fifteen-minute drive. They open at noon on the Sabbath and quickly fill their ten tables, so you might want to get there early. And, like the Brazos Belle, the Royers family doesn't accept credit cards, so take cash or a personal check.

FOR MORE ROMANCE

As you lazily wend your way back to Houston traveling east along US–290, you'll notice the signs for the **Nueces Canyon Equestrian Center** (8 miles west of Brenham, on 290; 979–289–5600 or

800–925–5058) on the right, before you reach Brenham. This is your chance to see real Texas cutting horses in action, as competitions are held most weekends and you're welcome to watch. Admission is free to stroll the parklike grounds or "spoon" in the picturesque gazebo; and the Western-themed gift shop is a great place to grab some last-minute souvenirs of your romantic weekend.

The Sound of Music at Round Top

T INY LITTLE ROUND TOP—population eighty-one, the smallest incorporated town in Texas—packs an artistic and musical whammy that belies its diminutive size. The town has been chosen one of America's "best small art towns," we'll have you know, largely thanks to the Festival-Institute's impressive program of classical music concerts, but the village is also home to the state's finest antiques fairs twice a year, numerous art festivals, and live Shakespeare on the boards.

The pastoral countryside around Round Top is remote enough that you two will really feel as if you've escaped the big city, but not so rustic that you'll feel deprived of urban amenities like excellent food, cushy accommodations, and stimulating conversation. And those rolling green hills beckon exploring by bicycle.

Getting there is easy, though Round Top may not appear on your Texas map. It's only 75 miles northwest of Houston: Follow US–290 west toward Austin; then, 3 miles past Burton, exit Highway 237 for Round Top, which is about 8 miles down the road.

PRACTICAL NOTES: Round Top is most popular in April and October, when thousands of collectors and dealers in antiques flock here from all over the country for the **Round Top Antiques Fairs**. The fairs are held on the first full weekends of April and October (unless Easter falls on the first April weekend, in which case the spring fair is moved to the following weekend). For more information see the fair's Web site at www.roundtopantiquesfair.com or call (281) 493–5501; if you plan to attend, be sure to make your reservations *long* in advance.

Romance
AT A GLANCE

♦ *Attain a state of bucolic bliss at the* **Heart of My Heart Ranch** *(403 Florida Chapel Road; 800–327–1242) by frolicking on the lake, in the black-stone pool, or by the creek.*

♦ *Feel like one of the family—and enjoy a gourmet meal—at* **Royer's Round Top Café** *(Mill Street; 979–249–3611).*

♦ *Spend your morning cycling through the countryside; then pack a picnic lunch on the ranch or in the town. Lazily shop your way around Round Top's quaint village square in the afternoon.*

♦ *After a country-style feast at* **Klump's Restaurant** *(on the square; 979–249–5696), thrill to the music of the spheres at* **Festival Hill** *(Highway 237 at Jaster Road; 979–249–3129).*

The summer concert series at the Festival-Institute at Round Top has been rated as one of the twelve best summer arts festivals in the world. The June–July season features nineteen concerts, but music resounds at Festival Hill year-round. The annual concert total approaches fifty when you add in the August-to-April series, the Early Music Festival, and other programs. The repertoire ranges from ancient to contemporary, including orchestral, chamber music, choral, vocal, brass, woodwind, and solo performances. Even when the music stops, you'll still find plenty to do at Festival Hill: Their regularly scheduled Herb Days programs include lectures, garden tours, and delectable three-course meals.

For more information see the organization's Web site at www.fais.net/~festinst or call (979) 249–3129 for concert advice; call (979) 249–5283 for herbal events.

DAY ONE: afternoon

Make your getaway from Houston to arrive at your home away from home this weekend by mid-afternoon. Check-in time at the **Heart of My Heart Ranch** (403 Florida Chapel Road; 800–327–1242; $135 to $225) is 3:00 P.M. From the flashing light at Round Top's town square, continue on Highway 237 about 1 mile and then turn left on Florida Chapel Road. When the road curves, you'll see the iron gates of the ranch.

You'll want the extra time to fully appreciate this spread in the sunshine, to wander around the peaceful orchards and gardens before sunset. Stroll by the gorgeous black-rock swimming pool or hike through the woods to the creek that runs across the property. Innkeepers Frances and Bill Harris will be delighted to show you around and will even introduce you to their darling burros.

In the main house we like the Honeymoon Suite ($225) for its queen-size four-poster bed, sitting room with fireplace, and graceful French doors that lead to your own private porch. Granny's Cottage ($175) is wonderfully secluded, just down the footpath from the main house and close to the black-rock swimming pool. You'll fall in love with its canopy bed, thickly draped in white lace, as well as the double-jetted whirlpool tub. Both accommodations are available as a three-night "honeymoon package," complete with champagne, fresh flowers, campfire cookout and gourmet picnic lunch, plus breakfast in bed with heart-shaped waffles.

DAY ONE: evening

DINNER

Tonight you'll drive back into town for a gourmet meal at **Royer's Round Top Café** (Mill Street; 979–249–3611; moderate), beloved of locals and tourists alike. You really can't miss the cafe's distinctive facade that faces onto the town square; painted red, white, and gray, it resembles nothing so much as a cheerful Art Deco service station.

You'll love the Awesome Pasta, a plateful of fettuccine, fresh shrimp, and veggies tossed in a garlicky cream sauce, or the grilled pork tenderloin sweetly glazed with peach and black pepper. The French fries here are hand-cut, and the jalapeño bread served with homemade soups is divine. But the real star of the show is the pie collection, lined up ready and waiting on the counter. Shall it be a luscious fruit pie for you and your loved one—cherry, apple, peach, or blueberry? Or the decadently rich pecan, buttermilk, or "sinnamon roll"? Perhaps you two should settle for the tried-and-true, award-winning chocolate Tollhouse pie that's the calling card of this quaint cafe. Remember, at Royer's it costs extra if you *don't* have a huge scoop of ice cream on your pie; and also bear in mind this is another no-plastic destination, so bring cash or a personal check.

After dinner hang around long enough to check out the gourmet gifts for sale: pickled peppers, flavored vinegars, or Royer's clever "Café in a Can" that bundles a selection of the trademark cafe seasonings, preserves, and marinades into a gift-wrapped tin can. Check out the cafe's own cookbook, too, which captures both the loving relationships and the recipes of the Royers clan.

DAY TWO: morning

BREAKFAST

Breakfast is served this morning on the porch of the main house, if it's sunny enough; otherwise, join your fellow "ranchers" in the formal dining room. Almost all of them, you'll find, are lovers like you, a happy mix of honeymooners and golden anniversaries.

Then we recommend you borrow two of the inn's bicycles for a free-ranging ride through the neighboring hills and dales. These narrow country roads are perfect for cyclists: They're paved, but don't carry enough traffic to threaten life and limb. Do, however, watch out for the occasional cattleguard. Ask the Harrises to suggest a pretty route to follow, or strike out on your own to explore. Be sure to pack a camera for your morning ramble—this countryside is absolutely jammed with great photo opportunities.

DAY TWO: afternoon

LUNCH

When you return to Heart of My Heart, you two will have worked up a healthy glow and a hearty appetite. Take time for a refreshing dip in the pool; then pick up your gourmet picnic lunch from the kitchen. (If you're staying on one of the honeymoon packages, this delightful fare is included in your weekend price; if not, it's only a nominal fee.)

You can picnic just about anywhere your hearts desire on the ranch grounds or tote your basket back into town to kick off an afternoon's lazy shopping. The historical exhibit at **Henkel Square** (just off Round Top's main square; 979–249–3308), a wide, grassy area enclosed by split-rail fencing, is a wonderful place to spread your blanket, right under the noses of the llamas grazing placidly in the next field. Before lunch browse the eclectic collection of wines and cigars at the **Apothecary** shop at the entrance to the museum village; after lunch, you can explore the sixteen restored settlers' homes and then shop your way around the rest of Round Top's main square.

Next to Henkel Square you'll find two charming art and antiques stores: **Nellie's** (979–249–5322) and **Painted Pony Antiques** (979–249–5711), a co-op of several Texas dealers. Next door to Royer's Café is **Porch Office Antiques** (979–249–5594), with an interesting selection of quilts and china. More antiques and yummy homemade fudge are on offer at the white, barnlike **Round Top General Store** (979– 249–3600) on the other side of the village square.

Heading back on Highway 237 toward the ranch, look for folk artist **P. J. Hornberger's** house (205 South Washington; 979–249–5955). Even if she's not home, it's worth the peek into her sculpture-populated backyard; her gallery is that tiny shedlike building painted deep barn red. Just past P.J.'s you'll notice the charming stone cottage labeled **Herb Haus**—one of three shops clustered at **Round Top Inn** (979–249–5888)—selling culinary and decorative herbs. The 2-block compound is a worthwhile stop.

DAY TWO: evening

DINNER

Tonight you'll dine in the unapologetically rustic environs of **Klump's Restaurant** (on the square; 979–249–5696), with as many locals as tourists for company, most nights. The cheery red-and-white checked curtains balance out those dusty deer trophies hanging on the walls. Every night there's a different steak special on the aw-shucks simple menu, but we're quite fond of the fried catfish and the succulent barbecued beef brisket.

Afterward you'll head out to the Festival-Institute for an evening of sublime music. To reach **Festival Hill** (Highway 237 at Jaster Road;

979–249–3129), just head back north along Highway 237 for about 5 blocks and follow the turnoff signs for Jaster Road on the left.

The 200-acre Festival Hill grounds are beautifully landscaped with exotic and native trees, stone bridges, and splashing fountains, worth a visit for their own sake. If there's time before the show starts, stroll over to see the **Edythe Bates Old Chapel,** a former Methodist Church built in 1883 and magically transplanted here. Can you imagine a more romantic setting for a wedding? Through the avenue of trees, you'll see the Gothic Revival **Menke House,** built in 1902, a marvel of elaborate carpentry inside. Most concerts are held in the impressive, gabled-roof main building, the **Festival Concert Hall,** which seats about 1,200 music lovers. Be sure to look up to admire the intricate ceiling patterned with inlaid wood; then concentrate on the glow that music appreciation brings to your lover's cheeks.

As a memento of this magical night when "music and moonlight and feeling/Are one," you can purchase recordings of the Festival orchestra. Romantic selections include Chopin Piano Concerto in E, op.11, and Prokofiev Piano Concerto no. 3 in C; and Dan Welcher Piano Concerto no. 1 ("Shiva's Drum") and Saint-Saens Piano Concerto no. 2 in G, op.22. Music lovers take note: The "Shiva's Drum" concerto was commissioned by the Festival-Institute in honor of its twenty-fifth anniversary. You can order these cassettes by mail, by phone, by fax and/or e-mail (The International Festival-Institute, P.O. Drawer 89, Round Top, TX 78954-0089; telephone 979–249–3129, fax 979–249–5078, or e-mail festinst@fais.net). And it's especially heartwarming to know that all proceeds are contributed to scholarship funds for young artists.

Back at the ranch dare to take a midnight dip in the pool or embrace in the warm swirling waters of the whirlpool. No doubt you'll have the starry sky and the quiet night to yourselves.

DAY THREE: morning

BREAKFAST

Sleep in this morning and wake to sunshine, hot coffee, and another hearty breakfast at the main house. Bid your fellow lovebirds adieu and set out for the **Winedale Historical Center** (FM–1457;

979–278–3530). From Round Top's main square, follow the signs directing you to FM–1457; the center is only about 4 miles away.

Houston's beloved philanthropist, Miss Ima Hogg, donated this 215-acre outdoor museum site to the University of Texas. On the hillside above pretty little Lake Winedale, you'll find period-furnished farmhouses dating from the 1850s and a log barn originally built in 1894, which now houses the Shakespearean productions of the university's theater students during the summer months. (For more information on Shakespeare at Winedale, write to Parlin Hall 108, The University of Texas, Austin, TX 78712 or call 979–249–4099.) Guided tours on weekends are a mere $3.00, and the indulgent docents may let you proclaim your love from that marvelous stage.

FOR MORE ROMANCE

On your way back to US–290 and Houston, pick up some of those Royer's pies to take home. We're told that the chocolate chip, pecan, buttermilk, and buttermilk-delight versions freeze exceptionally well. As the wag wrote on Royer's wall, "Life's too short to eat store-bought pie crusts." Indeed! A year from today, you could solemnly serve one of those pies to commemorate the first anniversary of this weekend's love feast . . . or better yet, return to collect one in person.

Country Pleasures in Chappell Hill

T HE QUIET HAMLET OF CHAPPELL HILL is only 60 miles northwest of Houston and boasts many of the advantages of Brenham and Round Top—breathtaking vistas, rural peace, quaint shops, and hearty food—without nearly as much of the crowd. Once known as the "Athens of Texas," the community has maintained many of its Greek Revival plantation homes and much of its gracious Southern ambience. Outside of bluebonnet festivities, though, there's very little going on in Chappell Hill; but of course that's exactly the way the locals and out-of-town admirers both want it.

From Houston take US–290 northwest toward Austin. Turn right at the HISTORIC CHAPPELL HILL marker at FM–1155. Drive a few blocks and you're in the heart of "downtown" Chappell Hill. Don't blink; you might miss it!

PRACTICAL NOTES: Chappell Hill's **Bluebonnet Festival**, which is traditionally held the first full weekend in April, features an arts-and-crafts show, bluegrass music, and festival foods. It has the honor of being the official bluebonnet festival of Texas, as locals are quick to point out. Call the Chappell Hill Chamber of Commerce at (979) 277–1122 for more information.

Since this community is so close to Round Top and Brenham, it also reaches critical mass during the Round Top Antiques Fairs in spring and fall. If you're truly seeking respite from the hustle and bustle of Houston, the best time to visit is anytime *but* then.

♦ Pretend you're Tara's most famous lovers returned at the **Browning Plantation** (Route 1; 979–836–6144 or 888–912–6144). Pleasure your beloved with fresh flowers, a basket of fruit, or a muscle-smoothing massage.

♦ Dine on well-marbled steaks at Chappell Hill's newest restaurant, **Pastorini's Steak House** (FM–1155 and US–290; 979–836–7777).

♦ Poke around Chappell Hill's main drag, peeking into the museum, antiques stores, and a bona fide cigar emporium; then tuck into a heaping helping of country cooking at **Bevers Kitchen** (Main Street; 979–836–4178).

♦ After lunch work off those carbohydrates with a pleasantly hilly bike ride to the **Masonic Cemetery,** where you can look for families of Texas heroes.

♦ Travel farther afield for your supper at **K-Bob's Steakhouse** just off US–290 West in Brenham (2120 US–290 West; 979–836–7990); after, make like a first date and take in a movie at the **Westwood Cinema III** (2100 US–290 West; 979–836–7656) right behind it.

♦ Wind up your weekend with a vigorous horseback ride over green hills and dales. On your way home stop at the **Chappell Hill Sausage Company** (US–290; 979–836–5830) for hot, smoky links to go.

And since we've never been able to locate bicycle rentals anywhere in the county, best bring your own bikes if you plan to ride.

DAY ONE: afternoon

You'll feel just like Scarlett and Rhett from the moment you lay eyes on the **Browning Plantation** (Route 1; 979–836–6144 or 888–912–6144; $125), a three-story antebellum mansion that looks like a frosty white wedding cake snuggled in acres of velvety green grass. To get to the mansion, turn left (south) on FM–1155 and follow it for ¾ mile.

All four guest rooms are on the second story of the plantation house, and all are a generous 20 feet by 20 feet, we'd estimate, separated by a wide, formal gallery. It's hard to pick a favorite, as you'll soon see, but if we were forced to choose, it would be the sea-green shadiness of the Ships and Lighthouses room. It's got a great private balcony, too. Does your beloved favor a special flower? Then be sure to let your innkeepers know: They will place a special arrangement or a gift basket in the room awaiting your arrival.

For an even more memorable treat, make advance arrangements for a session with the local massage therapist for your first afternoon in the country. For $60 each she will work all those city strains and stresses right out of your aching muscles, leaving you both relaxed and in the mood for a loving weekend.

DAY ONE: evening

DINNER

You needn't stray too far from home for dinner tonight, as the best and closest meal is found at the newly opened **Pastorini's Steak House** (FM-1155 and US-290). Owner Dan Pastorini, you may recall, once played professional football for the Houston Oilers (who are now the Tennessee Titans, but there's no need to get into all that). He has since become one of Chappell Hill's favorite city-slicker transplants and serves the community as a volunteer fireman. At his restaurant you'll find an elemental NFL-style menu of thick steaks, fresh vegetables, and crusty bread. Now really, what more could you ask?

Stargazing for Lovers

Perhaps that astrological pickup line "What's your sign?" was ruined forever by the lounge lizards of the disco generation, but "Where's your sign?" is another question entirely. With the aid of a simple constellation guide and your naked eyes, you two can learn to locate each other's birth signs in the heavens above. You'll rarely get a brighter, clearer glimpse of the night sky than way out here in the country, so why not give it a try?

Back on the plantation rock gently in adjoining wicker chairs on your private balcony. Peel each other grapes from the fruit basket, if you like. Smell the sweet country air, admire the stars, listen to the crickets. You two have officially begun to relax, haven't you? Then you know what comes next . . . naturally.

DAY TWO: morning

Start your morning at first light with a climb up to the widow's walk that crowns the mansion. You'll be richly rewarded, we promise, with the spectacular sunrise view over miles and miles of rich green fields. While you're up there, poke around in those funny men's and women's dressing rooms in the third-floor attic space; the headless dressmaker's dummies will never tell if you steal a kiss or two.

Then thunder like eager children down the stairs for a hearty, country-style breakfast in the paneled dining room. As soon as you've polished off your last pancake, you'll set out to explore the tiny hub of Chappell Hill, on bicycles, if you brought them, or afoot, if you prefer.

Obedient tourists that you are, you should probably start your sojourn at the red-brick **Chappell Hill Historical Society Museum** (Main Street; 979–836–6033) for a quick study of the area's history, defined for the most part by cotton and tobacco planters migrating from the deep South. For a more playful look at history, make your next stop **Rock-N-Roll Antiques** (Main Street; 979–836–5627), where Elvis has definitely not left the building. Need blue suede shoes, a classic jukebox, a matched pair of soda pulls, or your own glass-topped gasoline pump? This is the place to find it. More prim and proper antiques can be found at **Evan's Antiques** (Main and Cedar; 979–277–9141) and **Hackberry Tree Antiques** (Main and Chestnut; 979–836–9515).

Across the street at the **Texana Cigar Company** (5080 Main Street; 888–4–CIGAR–4), you're likely to find the most authentic cigar-store cowboy you've ever seen, if owner Donnie Roberts is about. Last we saw him, he was wearing a ten-gallon hat, fringed buckskin jacket, and soft, knee-high Apache boots. This fragrant, old-timey store rolls its own cigars, but also sells gourmet coffee beans and spicy beef jerky.

DAY TWO: afternoon

LUNCH

 Hungry yet? Then wander east along Main Street to **Bevers Kitchen** (Main Street; 979–836–4178; inexpensive). Expect a heaping helping of hospitality and chicken-fried steak or Texas chili from these friendly folks, in a room warmed in wintertime by an authentic wood-burning stove. And, like every other cafe in the county, it seems, Bevers is supremely proud of its pies. Its kitchen rests its reputation on a righteous, fudgy version of pecan, so be sure to spoon-feed each other a fair portion.

After lunch you'll head north on FM–84 to find the **Masonic Cemetery;** just follow the signs from Main Street. It's an exhilarating bicycle ride on a roller-coaster road and an honorable opportunity to work off that extra slice of pie. Or you could drive, of course. The four-acre cemetery is prettily maintained and shaded by shaggy Texas cedar trees. As a bonus, you and your lover can see how many famous Texas families you find buried here. Hint: Do the names Davy Crockett or William Travis mean anything to you? No? Then for shame, it's back to the history books for you both.

DAY TWO: evening

DINNER

You've almost exhausted the culinary opportunities of tiny Chappell Hill, so tonight we recommend you travel at least as far as the "big city" of Brenham for your supper. The best-all-round dining in this area is at the **Brazos Belle** in Burton or **Royer's Round Top Café** in Round Top (see previous itineraries), but if you don't feel like driving quite that far, check out **K-Bob's Steakhouse** in Brenham (2120 US–290 West; 979–836–7990; inexpensive). The food may not win a gourmand's notice, but it's plentiful and fresh; if you fear you'll scream at the sight of another steak, they've also got chicken and seafood dishes.

The real benefit of dining at K-Bob's is that the new **Westwood Cinema III** (2100 US–290 West; 979–836–7656) is right behind it. If you two are starting to feel like a couple in the witness-protection program, maybe you've been out in the country too long. Heck, pretend it's your first date and go see a mushy movie. Hold hands, eat jujubes, maybe neck a little. You remember how this works, right?

DAY THREE: morning

BREAKFAST

There's time for one more hearty breakfast at the Browning Plantation, and this time you can justify your overindulgence with the notion of a brisk workout on horseback to follow.

Just ask your innkeepers to make arrangements with the nearby Shiloh Ranch for you. The owner trains wonderfully gentle horses that even the least experienced city slicker can ride in comfort, and he knows all the out-of-the-way trails to lead you along. Stick your camera in your pocket to capture this outdoorsy end to your romantic weekend, to relive once you're home. If you ever decide to go home—that is.

Let's say you do decide to return to the city, however reluctantly. There's one last stop worth making only 3 miles east along US–290, and that's the **Chappell Hill Sausage Company** (US–290; 979–836–5830). You can grab a hot sausage sandwich to go or buy paper packets of smoked links to take home with you. (Take our advice and skip the sausage-processing tour; it's way more information than you're likely to want.)

Special Indexes
ROMANTIC RESTAURANTS

Restaurant price categories in this index, represented by one to four dollar signs, designate the cost of an appetizer, an entree, dessert, and one cocktail for one person. The approximate price for each category is indicated in the following key:

Inexpensive ($): Less than $15
Moderate ($$): $15 to $25
Expensive ($$$): $25 to $35
Very Expensive ($$$$): $35 and up

ROMANTIC LODGINGS

DAYTIME DIVERSIONS

EVENING DIVERSIONS

General Index

About the Author

Margaret Luellen Briggs transplanted to Houston twenty-something years ago and has been thanking her lucky stars ever since. She is a restaurant reviewer for the *Houston Press,* editor for the Houston edition of the *Zagat Restaurant Guide,* and a contributor to *My Table* magazine. Her travel articles have appeared on Waterways.com and the *Houston Chronicle*'s Web site. Pursuing her master's degree in archaeology at University of Houston, Margaret spends her summers excavating Maya ruins deep in the jungles of Central America, but she is always grateful to return to the blessed bright lights of the big city.